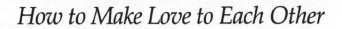

How to Make Love to Each Other

Also by Alexandra Penney

How to Make Love to a Man

HOW TO
Make Love
TO
Each Other

BY

Alexandra Penney

G. P. PUTNAM'S SONS   *New York*

Library of Congress Cataloging in Publication Data

Penney, Alexandra.
  How to make love to each other.

  1. Sex.   2. Love.   3. Intimacy (Psychology)
I. Title.
HQ21.P36 1982   306.7   82-18065
ISBN 0-399-12743-7

Printed in the United States of America

ACKNOWLEDGMENTS

Four special thank-yous: to Phyllis Grann, Publisher
and Editor-in-Chief Extraordinaire, to John Hawkins,
my exceptional agent, also to Howard Kaminsky, who
led the way . . .

And lastly, to Tuna B. Fish, the mysterious stranger
who continues to be a delight in my life.

Grateful thanks for their help go to Myrna Blyth,
Barbara Bonn, Paul Cohen, Nancy de Sotto, Alice
Fried, Ivo Lupis, Michael Martell, Dr. Allen Mead,
Marilyn Pelo, Suga, Larry Totah.

Immeasurable gratitude to all our friends for pulling
me through . . . and to the Cupping Room Café,
Elephant & Castle and the Beverly Hills Hotel for
providing coffee, a corner table and special service.

For
Norman F. Stevens, Jr.,
and
Susan Price

CONTENTS

Contents

1
THE RED DRESS

"It's really okay," Carol says, but he can hear the disappointment in her voice.

"It's not okay at all—it's our anniversary," he says, "but there's just no way I can get out of it—"

"Paul, please don't worry," she interrupts to reassure him. "I know how important she is as a client. What time are you meeting her?"

"She wants to have drinks at the Plaza in the Oak Room at six. I'll try and cut it short as possible."

"It's really okay," she says again. "I'll be waiting for you."

He hangs up the phone and wishes he could leave the office right now and head for home. Turning to look out the window he speculates on how cranky, demanding clients can be wiped off the face of the earth—permanently. Sitting at his desk again, he picks up a pencil, thrusts it into the electric sharpener and

hones the lead into a vicious point. He prepares two
more pencils and begins to attack a pile of law books,
making notes on a yellow pad as he quickly flips
through the pages.

It's six o'clock sharp and Paul, with his lawyer's
briefcase in one hand and a white shopping bag in the
other, searches the crowded Oak Room for his client,
an aging blond actress. She isn't at the bar—where
she'd be flirting with the bartender—nor is she at one
of the small marble-topped tables nearby. Hardly
hiding his exasperation and annoyance with the
command-performance meeting, he waits for her at the
entrance to the bar, reviewing the details of the case in
his mind while his foot taps impatiently.

"Mr. Hayes, paging Mr. Paul Hayes," the bellhop's
voice sounds loud and clear over the muted tones of
business-deal talk.

"You're to go to Room 1404," he explains when Paul
makes himself known.

As the elevator whisks upward Paul wonders what
the devil Nataly is up to now. A seduction scene
perhaps? Oh Lord, he thinks, save me. . . . His mind
flashes on Carol and the disappointment in her voice
when he had called.

"Come in," says a husky voice when he knocks at
the heavy door. "It's open."

Paul's first vision is of a raven-haired woman in a
black satin slip—the luxurious kind that French movie
stars wear. The woman has her back to him. She turns
slowly and dramatically.

"Carol! What are you doing here? Where's Nataly?"

"What do you think I'm doing here? Happy

12

Anniversary!" She can't hold back the laughter when
she sees his face. "Nataly's in Hollywood where she
belongs. I planned the whole hoax with your secretary.
I knew you'd never suspect. The children are at
Mother's and we have the entire night here!" Still
laughing, she kisses him and begins to slip off his
jacket.

"You're absolutely crazy and wonderful. It's the best
surprise," he says, laughing and collapsing on the bed.
"I love you so much—more than ever! And it's been
nine years!"

Half an hour later, sipping the last icy remnants of a
bottle of champagne, they stand with their arms
around each other to look at the magical view. The
almost-full moon looks like a giant faraway pearl and
the streetlights are strung like a diamond necklace
among the darkened trees of Central Park.

"Sparkles always remind me of you," says Paul,
walking back to the closet to get a square white box
from the shopping bag.

Fiery red sequins and beads catch the light and
glitter as she lifts the fabulous Twenties chemise from
the package.

"It's incredible! But are you sure this dress is legal?"
she asks seconds later as she models it in front of the
full-length gold-rimmed mirror.

"I'm the consenting adult who bought it," Paul says,
grinning at her. "The lady in the antique-clothes shop
told me it has mystical powers . . ." She interrupts
him with a deep kiss, and, as she moves her body to
curve into his, the beads of the dress glisten and turn
to a deep crimson in the soft light.

13

"And the powers are even greater when you take it off," he continues, slipping the dress over her hips.

She is unfastening his belt. "And your waist size hasn't even changed in all these years," she says with mock-envy and a seductive smile. He pretends to pay no attention to what she's doing and reaches down to her warmness. "*Your* waist—and everything else— looks just fine to me," he whispers as they begin to make love to each other . . .

Carol and Paul are not characters that a savvy script writer has dreamt up for a romantic TV series. I've known them for the nine years that they've been married—and three before. They have two children, two cars, two crazy beagles, two careers, and they live in a smallish town within commuting distance of New York. They may sound like the perfect twosome but, as a matter of fact, they have differing viewpoints on almost everything from politics to the way dishes should be done. Like everyone else, they have real problems, real conflicts, real insecurities and they argue—a lot—but unlike most people they have a committed, long-lasting, exciting, intense relationship with each other.

Once in a while they pull out all the stops, Carol steps into her red beaded dress, and they have a night on the town, but the majority of their evenings are spent at home with the children or with close friends. Carol and Paul like to be with each other, touch each other, share the good times and the bad. Paul once told me, "It's a tough, competitive world. It's all too easy to get off-track and think that money and careers or what schools the children go to are the most important things in life. Carol and I value each other and we value our children and our friends. We want to be together for richer or poorer, better or worse, in sickness or health—forever!"

Carol and Paul have a love relationship that really *works*—emotionally, spiritually and physically. They are among the many people—married, single, divorced, living together—that I interviewed in order to write this book. What makes certain relationships so special? What does it take to have an intensely committed, exciting, rich, long-lasting relationship? Before we get to the specific answers to these and many other questions, it's helpful to take a quick look at what's been happening over the past decade.

Looking Back . . . and Right Now

If you look back over the '70s you'll see scores of books and magazine articles devoted to what women needed, emotionally and physically. Women's roles in society changed rapidly, and both men and women were caught in the difficult process of redefining and reevaluating who they were and what they wanted. But the focus of the decade was primarily on women.

In the specific area of sexuality, the multitude of voices that resounded on television and radio as well as in serious books and periodicals, informed us that women were multi-orgasmic, that we needed a different sense of touch and timing, that we thrived on care, affection, romance and a special sensitivity to our psyches. Although there seemed to be an avalanche of material on the subject, much of the information was helpful, and real progress was made toward an understanding of female sexuality and a woman's physical and emotional needs.

The '80s started out with a burst of books devoted to the second sex—men. *Men in Love, The Hite Report, How to Make Love to a Man,* and a battery of articles in popular magazines began to give us a view of what contemporary men want and need in an intimate relationship. Research focused on men's fears and anxieties, their preferences and their peeves. Men had always been assigned the role of Prince Charming. They were to take a woman to dinner, order the proper wine, tip the maître d', and when all was said and done, they were *expected* to drive home and take the lead in the bedroom. Women began to find out that men didn't always like to play this role; a great many males were secretly—or openly—hoping for an equal partner who would take equal responsibility in lovemaking, a sexually knowledgeable woman who makes the first moves once in a while, if not fifty percent of the time.

Today, we're at a point where we can look back and begin to get some perspective. We've been through the "sexual revolution." We've been through "free" love, "open" marriage, and the what's-in-it-for-me attitude of the past decade. "The 'me' generation of the '70s is

evolving into the 'we' generation," says a well-known
New York psychologist I interviewed who works with
couples. "What people are anxiously looking for today
is a romantic, deep, nourishing—in a word, intimate—
relationship with another human being. Many of us
feel that this is most important and most valuable in
our unstable, unsettling, confusing world."

An architect puts it this way: "The relationship I'm
looking for is like a well-designed house: it warms you,
it protects you, it envelops you, but it allows you room
to breathe and grow." And an articulate 27-year-old
research assistant said, "I am so sick of keeping my
options open. Maybe total freedom is a trap itself. I'm
looking for something that lasts. I hope I'm not
searching for an impossible dream. I want to know
what makes people stay together—happily."

I wrote *How to Make Love to a Man* because I found
that women today needed specific information on
what men want physically and emotionally in a
relationship. The hundreds of letters I received and the
questions I was asked as I toured the country talking
about the book led the way to writing *How to Make Love
to Each Other*. The questions and letters took many
forms and came from women and men of all ages, 19
to 72, to be exact. What I found particularly striking
was that women consistently asked one type of
question and men were equally consistent in asking
another.

Women asked:

"How can I keep him interested?" "How can I

keep a relationship alive and exciting year after year?"

Men asked:

"Why doesn't she realize that good sex is important in making a relationship last?" "How can I get her to be more interested in sex?"

I think these questions reveal a great deal about the concerns and attitudes of men and women today—and the differences between them. These questions were the starting point for this book. I began interviewing married couples, live-together lovers and single men and women in order to find out the answers and to discover exactly what men and women want from a love relationship, what their ideas of intimacy might be, what their fears and hopes are, what makes the physical fireworks go off, what keeps couples together, what makes people stay in love, and what makes them drift apart. I also interviewed psychologists, sociologists and sex therapists, and read everything I could on the subject. In all, I talked to about 250 people of all ages and economic and educational backgrounds. They gave responses that were interesting, illuminating, poignant, surprising, and in many, many cases, highly practical and helpful for others.

How to Make Love to Each Other is an attempt to help both men and women to better understand each other sexually and emotionally. I've tried to give simple step-by-step physical and psychological guidelines in language that is neither coy nor clinical; above all, my aim has been to transmit clear, specific and useful information to men and women who are looking for a committed, meaningful relationship or for those who have one and want it to last.

2

WHAT MAKES
PEOPLE STAY IN LOVE?

What makes people stay in love? What makes certain
relationships exciting, intense and totally fulfilling?
What makes it possible to detour the divorce courts, to
avoid the bedroom blahs, to feel fully loved and
loving, to share your life with someone as an equal?

The answers lie in *intimacy*.

Intimacy is one of today's most overused, least
understood words. I talked with more than thirty men
and women from all walks of life trying to find a clear
definition, and the responses ranged all the way from
"lots of snuggling" to "cosmic closeness."

"Deep, profound," pertaining to or connected with
the "inmost nature or fundamental character" is how
the *Oxford Dictionary* defines it.

"Heart-revealing" was the way the poet Yeats put it.

"It's a situation in which anything is permissible," says a thoughtful cosmetics industry executive, "where two people are so secure with themselves and with each other they don't have to fake anything. They know that everything about them is loved—the good and the bad." This comes close—but there's more. "It's a love cocoon where we feel warm and protected and safe," say Carol and Paul, adding still another dimension to intimacy.

Having an intimate relationship—or intimacy—is one of the most wonderful things in the world, perhaps the most wonderful. Millions of people are looking for a close, committed, long-lasting, exciting connection with another person. But why are there so few of these kinds of relationships? Why is it that so few men and women have happy, exciting, interesting lives together? I think it's because many of us don't know what intimacy or an intimate relationship is really all about. We haven't really learned what it takes to have that deep, profound closeness that makes two lives rich and meaningful. "I want intimacy. Most of us do," concludes a man from Miami, "yet I just can't get a grip on what's expected from me. I think we have too many books and too few role models."

I've read books and articles on intimacy and I've interviewed men and women who have truly intimate relationships—and many, many more who don't—and I found that most people's ideas of intimacy are fuzzy or partial and that's a large part of the problem. You have to be very clear about what's needed if you want to have a relationship that gives each of you a feeling of profound connectedness, a feeling of great richness and fullness. Having an intimate relationship requires:

The ability to trust. If you trust a person—emotionally, sexually, morally, financially—you have a solid basis for intimacy. "It's extremely hard to trust in a total way, especially when so many of us have been taught from birth to be wary of other people and suspicious of their motives," points out a Chicago sociologist. Yet overcoming built-in mistrust—and taking a leap of faith to have complete trust—is essential if a relationship is to grow into a truly intimate one.

Honesty. You slam the door on the possibility of a meaningful relationship by lying or pretending. If you're faking orgasm or trying to please your husband by telling him what you think he wants to hear, you're on the wrong track. If you don't tell your lover or your wife that you need more sex or more understanding or if you tell her everything's okay but you're secretly seeing someone else, you don't have intimacy, you have a relationship of convenience. "At the heart of true intimacy is the truth," says a Houston man who cherishes the honesty of his eighteen-year marriage.

Time. We live in an enormously stressful world where everyone is hurried and worried, and if the moment comes to let the day's worries dissolve, a majority of Americans do so by watching HBO or the Jets or the Knicks or the Rams or *Love Boat*, instead of simply taking time to be with each other and talk with each other in a loving, intimate way. "Couples spend an average of seventeen minutes per week being intimate with each other," points out a New Orleans researcher. "People spend more time improving their backhand or daydreaming about an exciting relationship than in cultivating one." "Women have been raised to think they should do the dishes first. Intimacy is last on the list," says a reporter in San Francisco. And she's right.

Accept the other person's strengths and weaknesses. He can be a fierce, protective lion for his family and a great business executive but he doesn't know a car muffler from a carburetor and he gets unglued if he has to hang a painting; she is a warm, nurturing mother and a successful career woman but she draws a blank at balancing the checkbook or candying a yam. The point here is: love your partner for what he or she is, not what you wish or would like him or her to be.

A noncompetitive attitude. Many of us want to get ahead faster, better or more often than the next person. Intimacy is an area where competition can be highly destructive. It's not a case of who's right or who's better or who does or earns more, it's a matter of compromise, understanding, negotiating, sensitivity and, above all, respect for the other person. "John and Yoko were a good example," says one of their fans, "two highly competitive people who did not seem to compete with each other."

A commitment to sexuality. Sexual intimacy is only one part of true intimacy, but for many people, it is the area that causes the most bewildering and painful problems. A "commitment to sexuality" is one of the most important parts of an intimate relationship. This idea may need a little explaining. Sexual researchers (Masters and Johnson, in particular),

24

therapists, psychologists and couples who have enjoyed close physical intimacy over a long period of time agree that being committed to sexuality is a critical factor in keeping a marriage alive and vital. In plain language, this means that you must be a healthy, sexual, sensual being who enjoys giving and receiving pleasure. It's surprising how many people today still don't allow themselves to think or feel this way.

I've come to believe that some men and women are born with "the golden touch." They have a special something that their partners immediately respond to—and *stay* responsive to. This "special something" is an intuitive understanding of sexuality and sensuality. It's knowing things like how and when to touch, how to move, what to do with your body—in sum, how to pleasure another person in every sensual way. Although some lucky people are born with "it," others can learn to develop their own sensibilities to give pleasure to others—and to themselves. Think about cooking for a minute: without looking at a book, instinctively the "born" cook knows how to put a meal together so that it looks good and tastes even better. Others have to learn by following the recipes and measuring out all the ingredients carefully. Both methods work. What I'm trying to say is that you can *learn* to be sensual and sexual and to communicate what each of you wants and needs. And this is what much of *How to Make Love to Each Other* is all about because the physical/emotional part of a relationship is one of the strongest foundations of true and lasting intimacy.

3

THE GREAT DIVIDE:
How and Why Men and Women See Love and Sex in Very Different Ways

Men are much more likely than women to play around.
Women don't want sex for its own sake.
Men are inclined to want more than one woman.
Women don't want sex with a variety of partners.
Men are much more aroused by the sight of a naked body.

These are conclusions of an eminent sociobiologist named Donald Symons in a book titled *The Evolution of Human Sexuality*, published in 1979. This book literally raised an uproar. It was scorned as the ultimate macho manifesto, giving men pseudoscientific permission to indulge in promiscuous sex while keeping women in their traditional, stereotyped roles as monogamous keepers of home and hearth. Others hailed Symons as a serious, scholarly sociobiologist making an important contribution to the science of the sexes.

Is Symons right? Are men basically wanderers, cravers of indiscriminate sex? Are women fundamentally unable to experience sex for its own sake? Do they really prefer monogamy? No conclusive case has been made for Symons' theories; research on male/female differences is still at the embryonic stage and remains open to wide-ranging controversy. But it is becoming scientifically clearer and clearer that there are many fascinating differences—besides the obvious biological ones—between men and women.

The most recent research shows that males and females seem to experience the world differently, that girls excel in verbal ability, fine motor coordination and dexterity, while boys have a more visual/spatial orientation as well as a certain degree of mathematical excellence and a higher level of aggression. (Many of these studies, incidentally, are being aggressively pursued by women.) Baby girls seem to have a special propensity for faces and are more likely to be sensitive to sound. Infant boys are thought to respond more than girls to lights, patterns and three-dimensional objects.

An important and intriguing difference between adult men and women is their differing reactions to visual material. Many women that I talked to do not understand how the sight of a nude body or an erotic picture can be such a powerful sexual stimulus to a man. Men who are interested in watching women in scanty bikinis, who linger over the pages of *Playboy* or who occasionally watch the seamier side of cable television are not innately "dirty" or coarse or crude. Men are highly responsive to visual input from infancy onward, and it may yet be confirmed that biologically they need some visual stimulation in order to be aroused.

Since researchers have theorized that, as children, females respond to sounds and are more adept at reading, it's not surprising that a number of women I interviewed told me that although they did not feel particularly excited by visuals or pictures of a male nude body, they did become much more specifically aroused when reading or hearing erotic or pornographic stories. This may also help to explain why "romance" novels sell so exceptionally well to women.

Still another fundamental difference that can cause problems is that many men say they want sexual contact more than their wives or lovers. In a *Redbook* survey done in 1980 with 26,000 participants, the most commonly argued-about sexual topic was frequency of lovemaking. (The second was oral sex.) Among the couples I talked with who have maintained a high degree of sexual intimacy, this was *not* a major issue. "Two people who like making love with each other usually have no problems with frequency," was the way a happily married talk-show host in Seattle summed it up.

When I wrote *How to Make Love to a Man*, I emphasized that many men make a distinction between making love and having sex. This was one of the points that received many knowing nods of recognition from men in audiences and from the many male journalists and talk-show hosts who interviewed me on radio and television programs. Men, it seems, feel very strongly that women don't understand this duality in their sexual attitudes.

Sometimes men want to have sex and sometimes they want to make love. "Having sex is like having a good workout," describes Jeffrey, an electrical contractor from Boston. "You get sweaty, you feel better, you release tension. It either sets you up for the day or puts you right to sleep." Having sex, as I would define it, requires little caring or mutual concern, and it is most often a one-dimensional, one-sided, self-oriented, tension-relieving activity. Making love, on the other hand, is, for men as well as women, a multi-leveled, caring, giving experience that includes the physical act of intercourse but is far, far more. It is a complete experience that involves two people who are helping each other to reach emotional as well as physical fulfillment; in making love there is an essential feeling of having given and received. "It's rich, it's varied, it's complex and all-encompassing—and I want it to go on forever," is how a Baltimore woman described making love.

But aren't women capable of enjoying impersonal or casual sex?

"Before I saw *Looking for Mr. Goodbar*, I made a deal with myself to go out to a singles place, pick up a man and take him home with me," Jean, a 32-year-old assistant professor at an Ivy League school, told me. "I wanted to see if I could just fuck, no messy emotions attached. And I did precisely what I set out to do. I woke up feeling terrific, fed him some orange juice and sent him on his way. I never even knew his last name. Later on, I found myself saying, 'I got exactly what I wanted but why do I feel so bad?'" For Jean, nameless sex, for whatever reason, is unsatisfying sex, and for the majority of women I talked with, the same holds true; an emotional element seems to be necessary in intimate physical contact. A few women I interviewed reported they fully enjoy casual or fleeting sexual encounters, but my own suspicion is that many women wish they could more easily indulge in transient sex but find it difficult to do without feeling guilt, anxiety or emptiness.

How to Cross the Sexual Chasm

If men are sometimes or often interested in the joy of pure physical sex, if they respond to a plunging neckline, a bared behind or an overtly pornographic picture, and women react to a different set of stimuli, if men appear to need more sex and women seem to want "better" sex, is it possible for us to meet and mate in a satisfying way?

I think the answer lies in awareness and understanding of the differences in men's and women's attitudes as well as a keen sensitivity to the

31

needs of your individual lover. If, for example, you understand that men often feel strong needs for direct, undiluted physical sex, why not see what a turn-on it can be for you? Pure physical sex with someone you love can be a terrific experience if you don't add any emotional expectations to it—especially if you know that good give-and-take lovemaking is a major part of your sexual repertoire.

If you sense that your husband or lover is delighted with sexy underwear or responds to erotic pictures, why not be clever and use them to arouse him. If you're embarrassed or feel it's not your style, why not try and work out something that pleases him—and you too. I know a woman who feels ridiculous in black lacy underwear, but clad in a chaste white Victorian nightgown she delights in reading erotic novels to her lover—and later they both pore over the illustrations!

On the other side, men need to remember constantly that most women respond to the classically romantic: candles, flowers, tender gestures, murmured words (if you mean them)—these are treasured by most of us. "Having dinner with a man in a romantic restaurant is really a part of lovemaking," explains a divorced Minneapolis woman who has reentered the dating scene, "whereas most men think of it as something to be got through so they can get you in the sack." "I wish that more men knew that dancing is a form of foreplay," adds another woman. Dancing with her, singing to her, talking and laughing with her—the wise man understands how and why this—and more—makes a woman warmly responsive to him.

Whatever our inborn, cultural and sexual differences may be, there are intelligent, creative and affectionate ways to bridge our variances. Hopefully, this book will help to provide a starting point.

4

HIGH ANXIETY:
What We Fear Most in Love Relationships

"My deepest sexual fears? I'll never put them on tape. Call me between six and ten tonight," said the voice on my answering machine as I replayed the day's messages. The rather husky tones belong to my friend Barbara, who is one of the sexiest women I know. When she and I had dinner two nights before, I had asked her if I could interview her for this book and one of the questions I'd be posing to her was about women's fears in lovemaking. Her answers would, I was sure, be most interesting and enlightening.

I finished listening to the rest of the messages, took out my steno book and dialed Barbara's number.

"Okay," I said to her, my Rolling Writer pen poised in hand, "the world is ready for your revelations."

"You're going to be disappointed," she warned me. "I've thought a great deal about this and I concluded that I don't have any problems in making love—or having sex, since that's the distinction you always make. I love sex. I enjoy it. I've never had any hang-ups about it."

"Come on, B.," I said, "are you holding out on me? You must have *some* problems. We all do."

"Well," she said, hesitating. "Does this qualify? When I make love with Mark after we've had a huge dinner with lots of wine, I always worry that my stomach's going to rumble at the wrong moment."

Barbara is in her late thirties with beautiful skin, blue eyes and a wonderful mane of auburn hair. She is a serious, successful writer who favors crimson and yellow sweat pants and sneakers, has a tendency to a pot belly if she doesn't watch it, plays esoteric motets on her flute and, twice a week, visits elderly people to read to them. Definitely not your basic Marilyn Monroe type, yet a number of men who are mutual friends of ours have told me they find her exceptionally attractive—and exceptionally sexy. I'm convinced that one of the reasons Barbara is considered so appealing is that she is fear-less when it comes to lovemaking and she gives off a subtle aura that says she loves loving. "Listen," she says, "men and women were born to get together—what's to be afraid of?"

Men sense the self-confidence and uninhibited

feelings that she projects and they're attracted to her. Barbara is a woman who thoroughly enjoys her sexuality and feels no guilt about the pleasures it can bring. Unfortunately, women like Barbara are still in the minority.

For most of us, fear is a well-known bedfellow and it is fears, according to most sexual researchers and therapists, that are the greatest impediments to love and lovemaking. In talking with men and women, it's interesting to hear that each sex has such markedly different anxieties when it comes to sexuality. The following are the most common.

WOMEN'S SECRET PROBLEMS

This paragraph could as easily be titled "Fear of Pleasure" or "Uptight Upbringing." There are legions of women who still feel that there is something "dirty" or "bad" about enjoying sex. Barbara is a conspicuous example of the opposite feelings. Her natural ease with her body and her unprejudiced attitudes are some of the reasons that she has such a delightful time in making love. Although most of us know—in our *heads* —that good lovemaking is, or should be, a pleasurable, wonderful, enjoyable activity, in the stark reality behind the bedroom door, subversive feelings snipe at us: "Good girls shouldn't do *that* . . ." "He'll feel threatened if I do *this* . . ." or "He won't respect me if I want *that* . . ." Many books and articles have been written on the negative effects of leftover

Victorian attitudes and there are powerful forces still at work to convince some women that great sex is a great wrongdoing. The reasons behind these lingering attitudes are psychologically and socially complex, but for women who are still victims of this kind of unhealthy thinking, there is a way out: Give yourself permission to enjoy your own natural sexual responses. Don't do anything that you don't want to do or are uncomfortable with but keep an open mind and be experimental. This does not mean "kinky" sex, it simply means a willingness to experiment—as slowly as you need to—with removing the barriers, emotionally and physically, when you are making love. Tell your husband or lover that certain things make you anxious or fearful; the simple act of talking about your problems can do much to unravel them. If he wants to do something or wants you to do something which you feel is simply beyond your limits, tell him you're not ready for that—*yet*. It's not easy to keep an open mind and maintain a willing attitude, but it's necessary if you genuinely want to pleasure your partner—and yourself.

The Cellulite Complex

Because men's worst fears in an intimate situation are markedly different, it comes as a surprise to many men that body image is, for a majority of women, an especially vulnerable area.

"For many months after I was married, I backed out

of the shower so my husband wouldn't see my behind," admits a high-powered Detroit executive who, when clothed, appears to have an admirable backside. "I still am uncomfortable if he gets a direct view, so I always put a half-slip on first when I'm getting dressed . . ."

Many men would be surprised to hear this story, yet many women have told me similar tales about being embarrassed with their bodies. We worry about breast droop, waist size, thigh girth, creeping cellulite and almost everything else in between—including, of course, natural body odor and scents. In short, one of the strongest sexual fears among women is the fear of not being desirable enough. "Thank God, a wise man sensitively taught me that his lack of an erection was due to my naiveté in touching and arousing him, not the lack of my chest endowment," said one woman who grew up believing that men automatically have erections at the sight of beautiful female contours.

We all appreciate perfectly beautiful faces and bodies but it should be obvious that most of us have to live with our imperfect selves. Feeling comfortable with your own body is surely a prerequisite to feeling comfortable with someone else's.

"WILL HE THINK THAT I KNOW TOO MUCH?"

Some women fear that a man will think they are "easy" or have been promiscuous if they appear sexually knowledgeable. A case in point is the following:

"My first sexual experience was with my husband," recounts Carla, an energetic, attractive woman who teaches the sixth grade in Philadelphia. "At one point early in our marriage, John seemed to be very upset by the fact that I was good in bed. He even implied that I had lied to him about my virginity . . ."

"What did you do about this?" I asked.

"I told him that I'd read a marriage manual—which was only half the truth. Months later, when we were far more comfortable with each other, I was able to admit that I'd just done what I felt would be pleasurable to him. It took him a while to relax with me and realize that sex is also good for women."

Although some men find a sexually aware woman to be threatening, a majority of men that I interviewed expressed relief and pleasure at the discovery that a woman is skillful and knowledgeable about lovemaking. "It's terrific to know that you don't have to go through a lot of groping and moping because of crossed wires," pointed out a bachelor lawyer. "Men appreciate a woman who knows what she's doing."

THE AGGRESSION FACTOR

Many women worry that if they take the initiative in lovemaking, their partners will feel they're too forward, too aggressive, not feminine enough. I think the notion behind this theory is that a man's ego is too fragile to survive a direct hit on a traditionally masculine role—that of the dominant force in a sexual relationship. This kind of thinking is obviously flawed. Everyone's ego is fragile. It's more likely that the recent fluidity and changes in stereotyped roles are making both men and women anxious and unsure about what is "too aggressive" or "too passive."

Some men respond adversely to women who make the first moves in an intimate physical situation. These men may have deeper psychological problems underlying their attitudes. Most men told me that they prefer a woman who takes the initiative some of the time. "Some" is the key word: a woman who is doing all the courting and calling all the sexual shots is as unappealing to men as the woman who lies back and sighs, "Do what you need to do." A woman who says, "I feel like seducing you tonight" is far likelier to get a better reception than the one who demands action.

Precisely because male/female roles are undergoing such rapid change, it is a chancy business for a woman to know when and if she is being aggressive in an off-putting way. Perhaps the most helpful guideline to keep in mind is that most men today say they *want* a responsive, active and, above all, equal partner in the bedroom. If you've been married or living together for a long period of time and you would like to take a more active role in lovemaking, discuss it with your partner. Ask him if he might enjoy making some changes. Tell him you've read that men today seem to like more aggressive women—is he interested? If he is—and most men will be—you might suggest, as a first step, setting aside a special evening when he will be romantically—not aggressively—seduced by you.

Orgasms—One, Many, or None at All

Fear of not having an orgasm—or many orgasms—is precisely one of the greatest inhibitors of orgasm. Multitudes of women lament that they have never "achieved" multiple orgasms and they fear they never will. The idea of *achieving* anything in sexuality can be counterproductive. You don't get gold stars on your forehead for the number of orgasms you have. Achievement implies a goal and there are no specific "goals" in lovemaking. Research shows that some, not all, women have developed the capacity for multiple orgasms, thus, a woman may be multi-orgasmic or content with a single orgasm, or sometimes she enjoys lovemaking without an orgasm at all.

"How Can I Say What I Think or Tell Him What I Need Without Losing Him?"

Closely related to the fear of being overly aggressive is the anxiety women face in telling their husbands or lovers what they feel and need sexually. To be honest in any relationship is difficult and the anxieties are infinitely multiplied in an intimate situation. If the relationship has lasted over a period of years and certain issues have never been faced directly, many women feel it is impossible to be sincere and honest. Chapter 12, "Baring Your Souls," gives some helpful, specific ways to talk to your husband or lover about what you want and feel.

"I'M AFRAID HE'LL LEAVE ME . . ."

To a greater or lesser degree, we all fear being abandoned and all the women I interviewed admitted to having fears of being left alone. Of course, relationships change, people grow, they find new challenges, they leave each other, but things do not happen in a vacuum or without reason.

I know a woman who was totally surprised and nearly devastated when her husband of seven years left her for another woman. It's true that he bolted suddenly, but she had never really been conscious of the obvious clues he gave that the marriage—particularly in the sexual area—was not going well. And she herself had never admitted that many of her own needs, sexual and emotional, weren't being met. It was clear to almost everyone else who knew this couple well that the marriage was not working. Jan, the wife, was probably the only one surprised by her husband's sudden takeoff.

One New York therapist I talked with told me that she advises patients to make a periodic "updating" of their marriages. "People should take time to evaluate where they are, how they've grown or changed, how close they've become, or how far apart they've drifted," she explains. She counsels couples to do this at least once every year and more often if the relationship is undergoing rapid changes or is under particular stress.

Men's Greatest Fears

I think it's extremely difficult for a woman to accurately imagine the intense anxiety that a man faces in a sexual situation. We're all aware that men must "perform," that is, in order for sexual intercourse with penetration to occur, a man must have an erection. In an intimate situation, a man simply can't hide the fact that he is, or is not, ready to have intercourse. Until I began interviewing men about their fears, I had not fully realized the degree to which "performance anxiety," as it is psychologically labeled, affects them. It's surely the most sensitive area in the whole spectrum of male sexuality, and I think many women have only a vague idea of the problems it can cause.

For most men, sexual "performance" has come to be the ultimate manifestation of maleness and virility, and the ability or inability to perform is closely related to the deepest, most vulnerable reaches of the self. *"No man can will an erection,"* write sexual experts Masters and Johnson (the italics are theirs), and because of this unpredictable phenomenon a host of uniquely male fears and anxieties springs up. "It's a panicky feeling," says a San Diego real-estate broker, "because you never know if it's going to happen or not." Unfortunately, like fears about "achieving" orgasm, the more fears and anxieties a man has about performance or "achieving" an erection, the more likely it is that he won't be able to perform. Ways that these anxieties can be minimized will be discussed thoroughly in upcoming chapters.

Performance also implies a certain competitive

quality which is equally detrimental to lovemaking. A man wonders if he is a sufficiently skillful lover, if he pleases her as much as her ex-husband or ex-boyfriend. Closely linked to skill in a man's mind is the size of his penis. Here, too, there is an element of competition, although most men are embarrassed to admit it. "The size of a man's equipment," states one New Yorker whom I would classify as a thoroughly cerebral type, "even in our liberated society, is still a matter worthy of attention to most women—and men too, although you won't find them admitting to it."

Interestingly, I've found that most men suppose that women are fascinated by the size of a man's genitals and that female locker-room or luncheon chatter consists of detailed comparisons of masculine size, skill and staying power. For the record, the women I interviewed denied this. A notable exception, however, is the very attractive and very bright female editor-in-chief of a national magazine who asserted unequivocally over an elegant luncheon at New York's chic Côte Basque restaurant, "Size counts, there's no getting around it." Perhaps the truth on this minor but highly controversial issue lies somewhere in between.

If performance is the one intransigent male fear, its corollaries also cause great anxiety and it is important for women to be aware of them: fear of premature ejaculation, fear of being unable to maintain an erection, and fear of impotence.

Many men wonder if they are similar to other men sexually. They fear that their needs and desires are abnormal or even perverted. They wonder if they're asking for too much, or too little, from their wives or lovers. They fear they might be "sex-crazed" or "sex-driven" or that they are leaning toward kinkiness if they're interested in pursuing their fantasies and/or secret desires.

Some men also have a deep fear of homosexuality. Some men—and some women—may not be aware that there is an enormous spectrum of what is considered "normal" male heterosexuality and it certainly includes fantasies of gay sex or even homosexual experiences.

5
THE BIGGEST TURN-ONS

Many women imagine that men are immediately riveted by big breasts, small waistlines and firm, trim, rounded behinds, and just as many men fantasize that women are impressed and aroused by broad shoulders, "washboard" stomachs, or the quantitative aspect of genital equipment.

The fact is: what causes sexual arousal varies from person to person and is related to a myriad of changing emotional as well as purely physical factors. One woman I read about was passionately attracted to an unattractive writer because his bare skin smelled like new-mown hay. A Scottsdale man I interviewed is "crazy about young coltish women" and a Denver antiques store owner thinks that "intellectual Rubenesque types" are the ultimate inspirations of passion. Each person has his or her idea about what excites and intrigues them and even then those responses can change at any time, thus, unfortunately, there can be no absolutely sure-fire listing of turn-ons. However, certain ideas and phrases turn up time after time when men and women discuss what is most sexually appealing.

If you ask a man "what is a turn-on for you?" he'll most likely take longer than a woman to give you an answer. It seems that a man's thought process first sifts through the physical to get down to the less obvious, more emotional aspects that are meaningful to him. A law-school professor put it graphically: "Right away tits and ass flick through my mind . . . then come other things like knowing how to handle herself, knowing how to handle me." When one man, a construction foreman named Vincent, turned the tables and asked me, "Do you mean what turns me on for a quickie, or for the long haul, a marriage relationship?" I realized that male double-think applies in this area too. "Both," I answered, noticing he wore a wide gold wedding band. "Well," he allowed, "a woman named Rita turns me on." "How?" I persisted. "Is she your girlfriend or is she your wife?" "She's *both*," he answered with a big wink and a delightful grin, "and *that's* how she turns me on."

I heard the words "feminine" and "female" many times over. When questioned more closely as to what this abstraction might mean, the nearest I could come to a definition was: "A woman who does whatever she has to do to make me feel like a man." This applies both physically and emotionally and runs the gamut from wearing satin bikini underpants and skillfully

executing oral sex to being able to pour afternoon tea.
A bearded blond cabinetmaker said, "I'm turned on by
a woman I feel I can take anywhere. I guess I'd call it
'natural class.'"

Summing up the various responses from married
and single men, I found that ninety percent describe a
woman who turns them on as being self-confident,
self-assured. Here are the kinds of words men use
most often when they talk about women who are
especially appealing for the "long haul," as Vincent so
succinctly stated it.

> self-confident/self-assured
> understanding
> sensitive/aware
> intelligent
> sensual
> subtle
> energetic/vital
> female, very female
> well-groomed
> fit

Predictably, women have quite different criteria
about what makes us take special note of a man. Many
women describe two kinds of turn-ons, but they're
quite different from a man's long-haul/short-haul way
of categorizing. "There's the in-bed type of turn-on
and the before-bed kind," says a thoughtful 30-year-
old Manhattan artist. "A man who's sure of himself is
terrifically attractive but *when we get into bed what really*

turns me on is his desire for me." I put her last words into italics because I heard them over and over and over again from women of all ages.

"I like a man who takes charge. Power is sexual," says a woman from Atlanta. "Men who can cry," says a doctor in Toronto, "are vulnerable and that's what most women are looking for in a man." "A sense of humor is a barometer of how a man is in bed. A man I was supposed to go on a blind date with called me last week to arrange a place for us to meet. He had no sense of humor at all and I could tell just by talking to him over the phone that he wasn't sexy," recounts a woman who echoes the almost universal female delight in a man's sense of humor. Here's what women think are the biggest turn-ons in a man, both before-bed and in-bed:

    smart/intelligent
    self-confident/self-assured
    romantic
    spontaneous
    understanding
    sensitive/vulnerable
    a communicator
    nurturing
    flexible
    affectionate
    sense of humor
    good hands

A comparison of lists, as you can see, is quite

revealing. Making a list of what turns you on about your mate and sharing it with him or her can do a great deal to reinforce the good points in your relationship—and can be a turn-on itself.

6
BARING YOUR BODIES

"The trouble started about the time that I stopped wearing knits and began to buy loose tunics to go over slacks. Then I caught on to some clever tricks so that Michael really wouldn't notice that I'd gained weight. I'd always get into bed first and lie on my back so that everything would sink down and my stomach would still look flat. Then I discovered that, lying down, my thighs would look thinner if I bent one knee and kept the other leg straight. On the beach I developed a great sitting maneuver so that I never had to slip out of my clothes standing up where everyone could see I was beginning to turn into the Pillsbury doughboy . . ."

Judy is 48 and her story is one of the world's most common. Ten to fifteen pounds of fat creeping up slowly over the years and Atkins, Stillman, Scarsdale and Southampton stop it only temporarily. Judy was worried that Michael, her husband of almost two decades, wouldn't find her desirable anymore. Had she ever thought of directly inquiring what he thought of her body? I wondered. No, she had not thought of it.

A few days later, a much-relieved Judy called with this report: "I asked Michael point-blank if he thought I had gained too much weight. I couldn't believe that he really didn't seem to mind. Sure, he'd noticed, but he told me that men like slightly pot bellies because they make such nice 'little pillows'!"

Many women are overly self-critical about the way they look. We tend to judge ourselves far too harshly about our body image. Why don't we check out reality by asking what our partners think about us? It would save a lot of unnecessary anguish. Judy found out that Michael loves her just as she is. "Most women live by the model mentality: thin is best. You'll find that men usually like a more solid woman. Marilyn Monroe never looked like the pages of *Vogue*," claims Michael, and many men affirm that they're definitely not as turned off by a few extra pounds of flesh as women so vividly imagine they are. "A man (or woman) who is hung up on the 'perfect' body is going to end up endlessly searching for an unreal, impossible perfection," says an extremely beautiful actress that I interviewed in Hollywood. "That person is only looking for a body, he's not looking for a relationship."

Suppose, however, that Michael, when asked, said that he preferred a thinner Judy. At least she then knows exactly what his feelings are—and it's up to her to take the responsibility to lose some weight permanently—if that's what *she* wants too.

Baring Your Bodies

Recently, I was a guest at a health spa in Florida. The luxurious gray marble and white tile facilities are segregated: men on one side, women on the other. Both sexes get together over lo-cal luxury dinners. One evening I brought up the subject of bare bodies, wondering aloud if men feel the same kinds of anxieties that women do.

The general consensus was that men face anxieties about their physical appearance but do not verbalize the problems as much as women—there doesn't seem to be the compulsion to go on and on about fat. One man, a Los Angeles television producer, admitted that he tried to avoid body exposure as much as possible. "When someone says 'Let's go to the beach,' I always say 'No thanks, I hate the sun,' or I make sure that everyone is a lot older than I am." Stomach paunch, underdeveloped chests and arms, scrawny legs and "love handles" were cited as particular areas of vulnerability. One of the instructors summed up the situation when he pointed out, "Today women are more likely to notice a man with pecs and they're turned on by trim butts. Everyone's really tuned into bodies because of the fitness craze."

It's sad to hear that many men and women make love with the lights off or with their pajamas and nightgowns on because they're anxious about how they look. We're all born with differing degrees of everything—brains, energy, sensitivity, good looks. "It's easier to accept your own body if you concentrate on loving it and taking care of it," says one practical San Diego therapist. "One or two nights a week sweating it out side by side on Nautilus machines can do wonders for a relationship," he observes with the greatest conviction, and adds, "Almost any exercise contributes to a heightened sensuality because you're more in touch with your body and your senses. This sensual awareness is especially important for good sex."

The following story should be an inspiration to women who have problems accepting their bodies. A close friend of mine, who is a well-known photographer, was shooting a series of fashion pictures on the island of Nantucket, off the New England shore, last summer. "I was doing some very sexy bikinis," he recounted, "and we decided to take a break for coffee. I walked up the beach to clear my head. Coming toward me from the opposite direction was a woman talking and laughing with a couple of teenagers. It was a very secluded beach, and like almost everyone else, she had on a bikini bottom and no top but she was different—she had had a mastectomy. Her stride was so self-confident and her upbeat attitude was so terrific that the operation was definitely a secondary issue."

The point is plain: It's not so much how your body looks, it's how you feel about it and how you transmit that message to others that counts. If you feel good about yourself, others are going to feel good about you, too.

7

THE FINE ARTS OF SEDUCTION

American's flight number 12 from Los Angeles was due to land in New York at 7:30 P.M. We would be at least a half-hour late, the pilot informed us in a standard semi-drawl. The airplanes over Kennedy Airport were stacked up, and we were maintaining a holding pattern. My cross-continental trip had been spent doggedly revising an article that was due at 9:30 A.M. the next morning. At the pilot's announcement, I began to feel the full impact of the past five days of hectic activity and the last four hours of cramped, intense rewriting. My back and shoulders were knotted and tight and my head was aching.

Finally, more than an hour later, the big 747 pulled up at the gate. I was dead tired and dreaded lugging my heavy suitcase off the plane and facing throngs of irritable Sunday-night travelers competing for taxis.

Walking down the ramp into the terminal, I

suddenly felt someone take the handle of my bag. I couldn't believe my eyes—it was my husband, Norman, who was giving me a huge kiss and guiding me through the sliding glass doors.

"What are you doing here?" I asked, totally surprised and delighted. "You said you'd be working late tonight."

"The job was canceled," he explained, "and I have a surprise for you." He was leading me toward a long, sleek car and signaling the driver to open the trunk for the luggage.

"What's this?" I asked. "What mad extravagance are you up to now?"

"Sit back and relax and tell me about your trip," he said.

By the time I had finished my litany of aggravations and frustrations and found out what was going on at home, I realized that we weren't going home. We had pulled up to a nondescript building on a nearly deserted street in midtown Manhattan, and I was being led by the hand to an old elevator which took us to the third floor. There was a discreet sign on the door but it was in Japanese. Totally mystified, I stepped into an entry hall, quiet and heavily carpeted, which gave on to a large square room with soft, subdued lighting and several leather sofas that were luxurious and inviting. A young woman in a short white uniform and black tights (no shoes) greeted us and asked what we'd like to drink. "Perrier, wine or a Scotch perhaps?" she offered.

"Where are we? What's going on here?" I asked Norman.

"You'll see," he replied in a mysterious tone.

I glimpsed two Japanese men leaving the elevator and being greeted by another young woman. I had the fleeting notion that for some incredible, exotic, unfathomable reason my husband had taken me to a bizarre brothel!

We sipped our drinks for about ten minutes, but Norman still had not divulged what would happen. The young woman returned and directed us, "Please come to change your clothing." She led the way to a small, square room with soft lights, a large mirror and lockers. She indicated two large towels on a shelf. I looked at Norman.

"To wrap yourself in," he said with a reassuring hug.

The young woman came back to escort us down a narrow corridor to a wooden door.

"Here," she said, opening the door to a small sauna.

Five minutes later, we were escorted to a rectangular room that was tiled—floor, ceiling and walls—in a pale seafoam green. Two tubs, small pools really, about five feet deep and five feet square, side by side, were filled with water.

"Start here, then there," the laconic young woman advised, pointing to each of the tubs in turn.

The first was filled with swirling, steaming water. Half-sitting, half-floating, we sipped at glasses of cool water, and I began to feel the knots of tension in my neck dissolving. I could have stayed there forever but a discreet knock outside signaled us to move to the adjoining tub.

We now plunged into cool, limpid water. After a few

minutes we wrapped ourselves in thick, fresh towels and waited to be led to our next Sybaritic destination.

In a narrow rectangular room were two cot-size tables draped with white sheets. A small shaded lamp on a black table cast dim light. Two women, both in white uniforms and black tights, motioned us to lie on the tables. They wrapped us in more towels.

What followed was sheer heaven. For the next hour we were kneaded, prodded, manipulated and rubbed in an Oriental shiatsu-type massage. The masseuses even walked on our backs, using their toes and body weight as massage instruments. The results: total relaxation, soreness and stiffness relieved, and a wonderful floating feeling of well-being.

Norman had taken me to an Asian-style health club often frequented by ballet dancers, athletes and people, like us, who just need to unwind after an especially difficult day or week. The experience at the health club included time-tested, classic methods for relieving emotional and physical stress and tension, all of which can be easily adapted by anyone for home use.

Unless you feel relaxed and comfortable, you're not going to enjoy making love. The following techniques contribute to a mental and physical loosening up. Use any or all as a bridge from stressful situations to a more relaxed, more pleasurable environment.

A soothing place. The lighting at the place I visited was soft and subdued and the attendants spoke in pleasant, hushed voices. Try to create an atmosphere of serenity and quiet in your bedroom; bright lights, rock music, television and ringing phones are counterproductive. If you can remove distractions such as these, you've taken the first step toward putting a smooth end on a rough day.

A drink. Take the time to sit together with a glass of iced water or herb tea or light wine. Stay away from discussions of business or family problems (this will take discipline), and stick to conversation about pleasant, noncontroversial subjects.

A bath or shower. Almost without exception, couples that I interviewed who have a high degree of sexual intimacy say they take baths or showers together as often as possible. Physiologically, warm or hot water helps to relax muscles and evaporate tension; psychologically, it generates a feeling of security and closeness. A tepid or cool shower following a warm bath helps to balance body temperature and contributes to greater relaxation. A bath becomes doubly pleasurable if you light several small candles, scent the water and listen to soothing music in the background.

A massage. Massage can be an end in itself or the perfect lead-in to loving. The benefits of massage as a prelude to love have been known for centuries, but it was the sexual researchers Masters and Johnson who actually underscored its therapeutic importance for couples today. In Masters and Johnson's clinics, couples who have sought help for sexual problems are brought through the various stages of sexual intimacy, beginning with a "non-demanding" stroking of the back, face, the arms, and the legs. This kind of relaxing, non-demanding, non-threatening stroking is simply a variation or combination of massage techniques that anyone can do.

There are many kinds of massage. Shiatsu, the ancient Oriental massage that I had after my California trip, is usually administered by an expert who has had many years of training. Swedish massage derives from Chinese techniques of physical manipulation and is also done by experts. However, with a little practice a novice can use the techniques of Swedish relaxing massage in combination with the very simple strokes of a sensuous or "love-massage."

There are five basic strokes (complete with French names) to a classic Swedish massage. Many experts recommend using a light lubricant such as baby oil or a scented body lotion. Start with the arms and proceed to the

> legs,
> chest,
> abdomen,
> backs of legs,
> back.

Here are the movements and how to do them. Use the strokes in the order given below and try to keep your hands in physical contact with your partner's body at all times. Many masseurs often start by lightly and reassuringly placing both hands on the stomach and then, without losing contact, moving lightly to the arms to begin the actual massage.

Effleurage. Using both your hands, make long,

gliding, even strokes proceeding in the direction of the heart.

Pétrissage. Using thumbs or hands, knead, press, and/or squeeze muscles using small circular movements.

Friction. Make circles toward the spine, pressing down with your palms. On arms and legs, use thumbs and fingertips and circle around the joints. Follow this with additional *effleurage.*

Tapotement. Make short, quick taps in rapid succession using either the flat of your hand, the side of your hand along the smallest finger as an edge, or your hands clenched as fists.

Vibration. Firmly place hands or fingers on body and vibrate by pressing and shaking rhythmically. Move quickly and evenly all over the body.

Combining or following these traditional strokes with a sensuous or love-massage is one of the secrets of great lovers. A sensuous massage simply involves long, smooth, loving, caring strokes, light pounding, kneading and rubbing of all parts of the body. The sensuous massage or the combination (Swedish/ sensuous) relaxes both your bodies, puts you in physical touch with each other, and, most important of all, takes the emphasis away from performance. The man who has erection problems will be grateful to the woman who takes the focus off his genitals and starts out by rubbing his back or kneading the tension knots out of his hands and feet. Women appreciate massage not only for its obvious relaxing benefits but also because it gives an extended physical contact which is often needed as a preliminary stage to sexual arousal.

The first stage of a simple, relaxing massage skirts any of the erogenous zones. You can stop there or proceed to the second stage which may, if you both wish, include more specifically erotic touching and stroking, in combination with traditional massage movements. Making steady, consistent, fluid movements relaxes the muscles and the entire body. Your rhythmic stroking and touching should not be interrupted, but may now begin to include the genitals and the breasts. Erogenous zones should be treated with gentleness and a delicate touch unless your lover requests otherwise. You may want to stop after you've given each other a complete massage, but more probably you'll want to go on and make love.

Quite a few men and women I talked with about massage brought up the problems of ticklishness. Ticklishness signals areas that are vulnerable or extremely sensitive. Pressing a little harder on a ticklish area often reduces the uncomfortable feeling, but if the spot is supersensitive, leave it alone or stroke only with permission. Tickling can be an aggressive act that yields a negative response: tightening and distrust.

A SIMPLE RELAXATION TECHNIQUE FOR TWO

Relaxation techniques are widely written about and most people are aware of them. However, I've included a simple one here because it is easy and pleasant for two people to do together. Use it as a way to relieve a stressful day, as a lead-in to lovemaking or massage, or as a way to fall asleep together more easily. The whole process takes about ten minutes.

Lie on a firm mattress or the floor, arms at your sides. Close your eyes and take a few deep breaths. First think about your feet. Forget everything else. Now mentally tell your feet to relax: "My feet are relaxing, getting heavy and loose . . ." Now move on to your ankles: "My ankles are relaxing, I'm letting them go." Then give the same directions to your lower legs, then your upper legs, concentrating on only one particular part of your body. Move on to your back, your abdomen, your shoulders, your upper arms, lower arms, hands and fingers. Finally, concentrate on your neck, your mouth, your eyes, your whole head, telling yourself each time to "Let go." Finally tell yourself that your whole body is relaxed and heavy, that you are completely still, warm and relaxed. Now count backwards from ten, relaxing your whole body more and more with each number. "Ten, I am relaxed, peaceful, my body is heavy. Nine, I let go more and more, . . . eight, I am at peace and relaxed . . ." and so on down until one. Stay still for a couple of minutes, breathing deeply and evenly and savoring the peace and calm that permeates your whole body.

You can also take turns doing this excercise. One partner gives the instructions ("Your feet are relaxing, getting heavy and loose . . .") to the other, speaking in a soothing, even voice. Some couples find this technique even more effective when accompanied by soft, relaxing music.

8
A TOUCHY SUBJECT

As I researched the material for this book I was constantly confronted—and surprised—by how differently men and women perceive and experience sexuality and lovemaking. The subject of touch brings these differences into especially sharp focus. If both sexes understand how we vary and how to meet each other's needs and, above all, how and where to touch each other, we'll be far more able to make love to each other in the fullest sense of the words.

Several decades ago research revealed that infants need to be touched, held and cuddled in order to survive. Recent research yields some equally interesting information: from six months on, girls are held and touched more often than boys. Some theorists speculate the reason for this is that a mother may not touch her son because she is subconsciously trying to avoid being seductive and that the father refrains from too much touching in order to "make a man" out of him. Other researchers feel there is sufficient evidence to state that women are tactilely more sensitive all over the body than men are. In other words, the girlchild or female *feels* touch more, is therefore more responsive to touching, and thus she wants more touching.

The amount of touching people do differs from culture to culture. Mediterraneans are constantly kissing and hugging. Most Americans tend not to. And it doesn't take a scientist to observe that small children, especially girls, like to touch their mothers and fathers a great deal but they are soon instructed verbally or nonverbally that this is unacceptable. We Americans seem to "program out" our innate sensuality and love of touch and replace it with codified, antiseptic, fleeting contact. It's interesting to note that beauty salons cater mostly to women. There we can satisfy ourselves with the sensuous experiences of hair-combing and cutting, massages, facials, manicures and pedicures—without feeling guilt. Most men, on the other hand, don't linger at the barber's; they're in and out of the chair as fast as they can be.

Touching can express warmth and closeness and leads to physical trust, which is one of the bases of intimacy. We need touching in order to communicate caring and affection and love and we need touching as simply a pleasurable end in itself . . . it's a basic means to just plain feeling good. When couples can learn to touch each other in the ways they each need, much of the anxiety about sexual problems—and some of the problems themselves—begin to disappear.

TOUCH TONALITIES

Touch falls into two categories:
- affectionate or nonsexual touching
- erotic or sexual touching

We begin to see clearly the differences between men and women in relation to these two kinds of touching. Most women distinguish between these two kinds of contact, that is, they separate sexual touch from affectionate touch in much the same way that men consciously or subconsciously differentiate between pure physical sex and making love. Most men don't realize that playful or affectionate touching, however, is central to most women's sexual responsiveness. Extended touching and kissing and cuddling all over the body—nonsexual touching—is as essential to most women's readiness to make love as is erotic or specifically breast/genital touching.

Many women feel that a man's touch contains a "demand" for sexual intercourse. Touching thus can elicit the opposite response from the one you desire. You're touching and stroking your partner, but instead of reacting with warmth, she is becoming increasingly unresponsive. Says one newly divorced woman of 38, "If I feel a man's touch as saying he wants 'more,' my body stops right there. I can tell he's not a good lover." The problem for a man, however, is that it's difficult for him, because of early psychological and social training, to touch a woman without some sort of "demand" in his caress. Before you can begin to erase the "demand" problem, take a look at how men feel about touching.

Many men are truly afraid of touching. Early training has led them to believe that they're "sissies" if they want to be touched or stroked or held, so it's not surprising that they shy away from giving, or receiving, nonsexual touching.

More revealing than fear of touch is the way that men respond to touching. Generally they perceive touch in sexual terms. If a woman hugs or embraces a man, he will not, as she does, think of it as a form of affection or warmth; he may take it as a prelude to sexual activity. Men tend to equate touching with a goal, the goal being sexual. To further complicate the problem, since most men prefer direct and immediate genital stimulation, they tend to think of playful, affectionate touching as a duty, as something to be done to "please" a woman. For many men, nonsexual touching is simply a series of stops along the way to genital touching, and this is exactly why women feel their touch is a "demand."

A Touchy Subject

WHAT WOMEN NEED/WHAT MEN NEED

Perhaps the best way to bridge the touch-gap is to explore exactly what it is that men and women need in the realm of the senses. Women need a great deal of touching, both sexual and nonsexual, and, from what they say, men are depressingly unable to satisfy their needs. Here are some very basic thoughts that should be of help to men.

- Women can immediately distinguish a grabby, demanding or aggressive touch from a warm, caring, affectionate one.
- Women need a great deal of affectionate touching. Imagine how much touching and cuddling and holding a woman might want and multiply that by three and you'll probably have a more accurate picture of the amount of physical contact many women would like.
- Most women prefer a light touch all over the body; as they become more sexually aroused the touch can intensify.
- Different kinds of touches and pressures are appropriate for different body spots, especially the breasts and genitals. An unvarying touch is perceived as mechanical and does not express sensitivity to the woman or her body.
- Response to touch varies enormously from woman to woman, and with the same woman it can vary from day to day and in lovemaking it can even vary from moment to moment.
- Touching doesn't stop with the end of

intercourse. Women need warm, affectionate touching after the sexual act as well as during and before it.

Anthropologist Margaret Mead, as well as more contemporary researchers have pointed out that *a woman's entire body can be erotically sensitive.* The lips, breasts and genitals are obvious erogenous zones, but almost every other area is responsive to caressing. Many women say that feet, hands and ears are often neglected by men. A good lover will take advantage of his knowledge that nearly every inch of a woman's body can be aroused by light kissing, blowing, licking or gentle biting.

The head is one of the most forgotten erogenous zones. One woman told me that the most seductive and erotic gesture her husband bestowed on her was brushing her long hair slowly and sensuously. Another sensitive lover gently caressed his wife's entire body with a soft sable brush commonly used to apply face powder. Another man, with an outrageous style, was reported by his fiancée, who recounts facts reliably, to have eaten raspberry jam off her toes in a San Francisco coffeehouse. "I was taken off-guard," she says, "but I had just had a pedicure and I loved it!" The imagination, sensitivity and spontaneity of this kind of touching is almost certain to increase a woman's receptivity to lovemaking!

The breasts and genital areas are perhaps the most misunderstood areas of touching. A woman's breasts must, at all times, be handled with sensitivity and care. Perhaps the most nearly comparable body area

72

for a man would be his testicles. Research has shown
conclusively that most women's breasts must be
caressed, kissed, stroked in a tender, loving, unhurried
way in order for the body to have time to begin its full
sexual response. Most men kiss, suck, stroke, rub, roll
and fondle the breasts and nipples for too short a time
and proceed immediately to the genital area as this is
the kind of routing *they* most prefer. It should be noted
that breasts come in all shapes and sizes, that it is a
normal reaction for the nipples to become erect when
stimulated (or if the temperature is too cold), that some
women who are perfectly healthy experience little
erotic pleasure from having their breasts caressed, that
most women prefer an even more delicate touch
preceding and during menstruation.

Much has been written about the clitoris as the
center of erotic sensation for women. Yet many
women today say that men still do not know how to
stimulate the clitoris in the ways that bring most
pleasure. The most common problem is a "heavy" or
"automatic" or "mechanical" touch. Sex therapists
point out that most women prefer an indirect approach
to clitoral stimulation, that is, stroking, kissing or
touching the outer and inner "lips" of the genitals first
and then stroking the right and left sides of the clitoral
shaft before touching it directly. It is important to be
aware that direct, prolonged concentration on the
clitoris can cause numbness and that, preceding
orgasm, the clitoris retracts under a hood of skin.
Change your type of stroking, especially in the early
stages of arousal, and continue stroking even though
the clitoris is retracted, unless your partner indicates

otherwise. Also, a lubricant is necessary to enjoy the full range of sensation from clitoral stimulation. If you don't feel enough natural lubrication, apply a small amount of unscented body lotion or K-Y Jelly directly to the entire vaginal area. Saliva is a readily available lubricant but many women point out that it dries too quickly.

The vaginal opening has many nerves and is sensitive to touch. In contrast to the opening, the internal walls of the vagina, which are supplied with fewer nerves, are not overly sensitive but are more responsive to pressure or thrusting. However, the controversial G-spot, thought to be a dime-sized area located on the anterior or front wall of the vagina, is said to be ultra-sensitive and, when stimulated, can produce an intense orgasm. The G-spot (named after a '40s gynecologist, Ernst Grafenberg) can be reached either through intercourse (particularly in the woman-on-top or "rear-entry" positions) or by inserting one or two fingers into the vagina and massaging the front wall up to and slightly over the ridge of the pubic bone. Exact location of the spot is unknown and indeed the G-spot itself is far from being universally acknowledged.

The outer surface of the anus can be a highly erogenous zone. Many women are extremely stimulated by a gentle rotating touch at the "bud" or entrance of the anus. When a woman is fully aroused and receptive, insertion of one or even two well-lubricated fingers and a slow in-and-out movement can produce intensely exciting stimulation. Since the anus has a long history of psychological and social taboos, some women (and men) may be against anal exploration altogether. Chapter 13, which discusses sexual negotiations, might be helpful in resolving differing attitudes and expectations in this still-controversial area.

Just as a majority of women report that they prefer a lighter, non-grabby touch, most men want and need a firmer, stronger touch—especially in the genital area.

As pointed out, either because of culture or biology, most men want women to give them sexual, i.e., genital, touching in the first stages of lovemaking, while women are more likely to desire the reverse. Some men aren't aware that a whole world of feeling exists in places other than the penis, but there are erogenous, or love-producing, zones all over a man's body. The following are among the most responsive spots:

    ears
    neck
    nipples (50–60 percent of men have a partial or full
      erection of the nipples when stimulated)
    buttocks
    inner surfaces of the thighs, especially near the
      genitals
    penis
    scrotum
    anus

Some general rules to remember when it comes to genital touching:

Most men like their penises to be stroked or held firmly. Keep in mind that the head of the penis is the most sensitive area and responds to varying degrees of stroking, touching or licking. The delicate vertical thread of skin on the underside that joins the head to the shaft gives a high degree of sensation, as does the long ridge, which looks like an engorged vein, that runs along the underside of the penis. The shaft has much less feeling to it; you can grip or clasp it very firmly. Men say most women do not hold the penis firmly enough when they are moving the outside skin of the penis up and down.

Some special erotic touches that men say they like include gentle hair-pulling, especially above the ears and close to the temples, biting of the tendons that run alongside the neck from ear to shoulder, gentle biting of the inner thighs, buttocks and especially the muscles that surround the underarm. One man reported an exceptional thrill from being lightly and rapidly nipped all over the body, with slightly harder bites running along the muscles at the top of his shoulders down to his nipples.

How to Find the Right Touch

Discussion, massage, trial and error—these are the most commonly used methods in trying to find the touch that your partner responds to most. A Los Angeles therapist uses another way that seems to work exceptionally well with the couples that she sees. What is involved is a simple role-reversal: each partner imagines that he or she is the other partner and then touches the other as she or he would like to be touched. You as the woman, for instance, would imagine that you are your husband or lover. You are giving him the sensations that *you* would be most responsive to. You, for instance, prefer long, sensuous stroking of your legs and inner thighs. You like your nipples to be sucked firmly, you enjoy the pressure of a palm placed above your pubic bone (many women do) while having your breasts caressed. Do these things to your partner so that he can experience as closely as possible what it is that feels good to you.

Now reverse the roles. You want your wife or lover to experience the way you would like to be touched. Perhaps you want much firmer stroking, much stronger holding, perhaps you like to have your nipples touched in a special way or you like to have the small of your back caressed with kisses—do these to your partner so that she can feel how and where you respond. You'll both find this simple role-reversal reveals a great deal as it shows specifically what kind of touch feels best without being threatening or arousing anxiety.

VIBRATORS

A vibrator isn't a substitute for human touch, it simply gives you another sensuous option. Both men and women are divided on the issue of vibrators. Some people love the feelings they produce, others are not so enthusiastic. The general consensus of dedicated users is that it takes experimenting with different types of vibrators to find the one that feels best. If you're timid or embarrassed about buying one, you can order through the mail-order catalogs for sexual aids you find advertised in national magazines such as *Playboy*.

Several couples mentioned the vibrators that are found in the small-appliance area of department stores. Promoted primarily as tension-relieving massagers, they run on electrical current and give a stronger pressure than the battery-operated kind. The hand-held massager with a small motor, the type used in barber shops, is also touted as giving a great variety of sensations.

You can use a vibrator to give a special kind of concentrated stimulation almost anywhere on the surface of the body, including of course, the most highly erogenous areas: breasts, nipples, clitoris, vaginal area, penis, scrotum and anal areas. Several men report intense stimulation from application to the anus and under the scrotum and women often use vibrators as an aid to developing multiple orgasms (see next chapter).

UNEXPURGATED GUIDE TO KISSING

"You'd be surprised at how many people don't know how—or where—to kiss," a sex therapist observed to me. *The Joy of Sex* says "a good mouth kiss should leave its recipient breathless but not asphyxiated (leave an airway open) and nobody likes their nose squashed into their face."

A Touchy Subject

Kissing involves mouth-to-mouth and mouth-to-body contact. It also implies intimacy (which is why many men never kiss prostitutes), but in today's rush to get into bed much of the exquisite art of kissing has been lost. Erotic kissing is a way of beginning lovemaking and is also another one of nature's prolonging devices; it gives women time to become aroused and it helps both partners become acquainted, or reacquainted, with each other's bodies.

A good kiss is described by both men and woman as

- somewhere between moist and too wet
- well-placed
- non-aggressive
- sensitive
- concentrated
- warm and giving

A number of men and women told me that today genital kissing is often considered obligatory. Nothing in sex should be an obligation. Genital kissing, as well as kissing of every other part of the body, is a sensual experience that is meant to give pleasure and warmth to the recipient. Fears of body odors are one of the deterrents to genital kissing. Sex therapists underscore that the natural scents of clean genitals are usually attractants to the opposite sex and that scented bathing or showering can, if desired, be incorporated into lovemaking itself.

"Kissing," sums up a Houston radio producer, "is nourishing, caring, healing, warming, loving. It's one of the most intimate exchanges that can take place between two people."

9
ORGASM UPDATE

If a curious Martian were to check out all the current books on sex, he would certainly be struck by the recurrence of one word: orgasm. Not until the mid-sixties when Masters and Johnson brought out the measuring devices and polygraphs did the word orgasm assume such preeminence on this planet. Ten years ago would you have heard a woman casually say, "I almost had an orgasm it was so good" in reference to a chocolate mousse served at a Chicago dinner party. Today, the pure concentration of the word in sex manuals, sex articles, sex therapy sessions—and dinner parties—is enough to make even an extraterrestrial aware that this is a Vastly Important Subject. Well, just how important are orgasms, what is the latest research in the field and how does it affect you? This chapter is all about orgasm, the peak of sexual excitement; it is intended to give information, to simplify the facts and help to resolve problems that many of us have faced at one point or another in regard to the "Big O." Here are the facts:

An orgasm is the climax of sexual excitement.

Both men and women have orgasms.

Orgasms are similar in both sexes. In fact, in a recent study in which people were asked to describe orgasms, the researchers could not tell whether the descriptions were written by men or by women.

Men usually ejaculate during orgasm.

Women *may* ejaculate, the data are not yet conclusive.

As of this writing, ejaculation for a man is still largely considered part of orgasm (although there is growing controversy about this), thus men seem to biologically need orgasm for the continuance of the race. Women don't need orgasms for any known biological reason.

It seems that women have a greater difficulty than men in having orgasm and that orgasm may indeed have a different emotional *meaning* for a woman than it does for a man.

For years debates have raged over "clitoral" or "vaginal" (and now G-spot) orgasms. The most widely accepted position today is simply: an orgasm is an orgasm—no matter how or where it is induced.

These are the up-to-date facts about multiple orgasms: since women are thought not to have a "refractory period" (the amount of time required for most men before they can regain an erection), they are capable of a continuing series of orgasms. The capacity for sequential or multiple orgasms usually develops

over months or years of practice, although some
women seem to have this facility intuitively.
"Multiple" may add up to two or three or as many as
fifteen or more peaks of excitement in one lovemaking
experience. Research is now focusing on the idea that
men can have multiple orgasms prior to ejaculation.
(Men cannot control erections but they can, with
practice, control ejaculation.)

Certain conditions seem to be necessary for men to
experience multiple orgasms. The primary one seems
to be the rate at which the penis loses its rigidity after
ejaculation. It might take one man half an hour to lose
an erection after intercourse is completed, while
another man's penis softens almost instantly. Up to
now, the differences have been thought to be inborn
and not controllable, thus the man with the slower rate
of detumescence may be more capable of multiple
orgasms. Some researchers also theorize that a man
may have multiple orgasms prior to ejaculation.

These are the most common problems having to do
with orgasms:

For women: difficulty in having orgasm

For men: premature ejaculation

Some women have never experienced one orgasm,
let alone a multiplicity of them. If you've never had an
orgasm during lovemaking, you might consider
consulting a sexual therapist who will work
comfortably with you (and your husband) to help you.
Treatment usually consists of several joint and/or
single sessions, focusing on defusing your anxieties
(past and present) and simple physical techniques to
achieve orgasm. If you've never experienced multiple

orgasms and you want to, a therapist should be able to help, but several women I spoke with reported that for them, developing the capacity for multiple orgasms consisted simply of masturbation to orgasm and then continuing stimulation after orgasm until another orgasm has occurred. Some therapists suggest using a vibrator to continue on to multiple orgasms and others suggest that, for many women, one orgasm may be all they want or need (or may be capable of).

By far the most common problem presented to sexual therapists is lack of orgasm for women during intercourse. For many if not most women, only clitoral stimulation leads to orgasm. In the past, doctors and researchers felt that unless a woman reached orgasm through intercourse, she was not functioning optimally. Therapists are finally convinced there's nothing "wrong" with a woman who cannot have orgasm from intercourse. Intercourse with manual and/or direct stimulation of the clitoris (such as in the woman-astride position), is often suggested to couples who are still worried by this.

Perhaps the most pernicious problem about orgasms is all the *emphasis* on them. For a woman, worrying about having an orgasm (like a man's worrying about having an erection) is the most direct route to *not* having one. One doctor I spoke with offered the following advice: "A book titled *Zen and the Art of Archery*," he explained intently, "holds in part that the best archers are ones who do not aim at the target. Don't try to remember all the 'techniques' involved in orgasm. You are not being judged, you are not in a kind of competition. Just as the archer is advised to concentrate his attention on the arrow, watching it, even listening to it, the best advice on having an orgasm is to concentrate on what is happening at the moment, not what may happen five seconds from now. Forget that orgasm exists and concentrate on the pleasure of making love. It's a simple principle but amazingly effective."

Even though a great deal of emphasis goes into orgasm, it need not be an inevitable part of every lovemaking experience. Many women find that often their husband's or lover's orgasm gives them an intense feeling of satisfaction. "I just don't come every time and I don't feel I need to. If I felt frustrated I'd know something was wrong, but I feel great when my husband comes and I don't *have* to," explains a Kansas City medical researcher. Psychologist and humanist Rollo May sums up this attitude more clearly when he points out, "Sex consists of stimulus and response; love is a sharing of one's being with another."

Although there is not enough specific evidence on the subject to be conclusive, several respected therapists and doctors believe that poor tone of the pubococcygeal (PC) muscle can inhibit orgasm and, conversely, keeping the PC muscle in shape enhances orgasm. The most widely used exercise for strengthening the PC muscle was developed by Dr. Arnold Kegel and consists in tightening and relaxing the muscle that is the same one used in stopping and starting the flow of urine.

For men the most common problem related to orgasm is premature ejaculation—and it can be treated with almost unfailingly good results! There are two

basic methods in general use today: one, the Semans'
stop-start technique, and two, the "squeeze" technique
advocated by Masters and Johnson, which is a variation
of the Semans' method. (For a version of the squeeze
technique, see page 97.) Both work and take relatively
little time to master. They have been written about
extensively in clinical and popular sex manuals but, if
persistent premature ejaculation is a problem, it is wisest
to consult with a therapist who will probably recommend
six to twelve treatment sessions (once or twice a week),
with both partners present. Ask your physician or
inquire at your local hospital for the name of a qualified
sex therapist.

WHY SEX OFTEN GETS BETTER
AS YOU GET OLDER

As we mellow over the decades, our timing
differences in lovemaking seem to equalize—and with
this come positive effects. As he gets older, and more
specifically after 50, a man needs more intense and
direct stimulation in order to become physically
aroused. Direct genital touching, either manually
and/or orally, is usually essential. Orgasms also
become less important as the refractory period (or the
time it takes to regain an erection) lengthens. These
changes can cause anxiety in a man or they can add up
to the good news that, since he's biologically slowing
down somewhat, he'll be more in tune with his
partner's needs.

Orgasm Update

The same timing and patterns of arousal still hold true for women as the years pass if she has had a fairly active sexual life. Although natural lubricants lessen after menopause, they can be supplemented with K-Y Jelly or non-fragranced body lotion and women regularly report heightened sexual enjoyment as they get older. Helen Singer Kaplan points out the fact that many women remain extremely interested in sexuality all their lives: 25 percent of 70-year-old women still masturbate.

According to some theories, as the years pass, men become more like women in that fantasy and mood are more important in lovemaking and there is less preoccupation with orgasm.

Lifelong lovers all seem to have one thing in common: they have been able to maintain high levels of sexual activity throughout their lives. In the off-the-record words of our researchers, "If they do it a lot they can still get it on a lot!" The slower responses that naturally occur over the years can be a true advantage—not only does it take more time to reach a high pitch of sexual excitement, once that peak is attained, many men and women in their fifties, sixties, seventies, and beyond, can maintain it for a very long time.

10
MAKING LOVE
TO EACH OTHER

WHEN

An Italian journalist who was visiting New York and greatly missed his wife once remarked to me, "Ah, eleven o'clock, think of all the people who are making love in this exciting city right now!" I reflected on all those people who faced the daily New York frustrations and indignities: hot, crowded subways, homicidal bus drivers, the cold, sleety rain, the dirty slush, the frenetic push to make a buck. Most of us are totally exhausted by eleven o'clock, but that's when the kids are finally in bed, the dishes are done and we have a few moments before sleep or insomnia sets in. It doesn't take much insight to see that late-night lovemaking may be less than ideal, yet many people always squeeze sex into the few bleary minutes at the end of a hectic day. It's no wonder that the experience is hurried, unsatisfactory and usually empty.

It can't be said often enough that *making love takes time*. Spontaneity is a terrific turn-on, but given the realities of the average two-paycheck household, it appears that planning for lovemaking might not be such a bad idea. Experts say that taking the time to rendezvous, instead of inhibiting sexuality, kindles it: in other words, planned lovemaking becomes something to look forward to. One couple I interviewed who were under exceptional career stress set the alarm back an hour several times a week in order to make love in the morning. "We realized that it was too easy for sex to go down the drain given the push we were both making professionally," explained Sally, "and if we don't make love we lose a vital connection with each other. Although it's a real drag for me to wake up earlier than usual, we decided it was the only solution to the problem until the pressures eased up at work for both of us."

"Some people think late-night sex is sexier and more romantic and maybe they're right, but I heartily recommend morning sex," says a Chicago psychologist. "A couple of drinks, a heavy dinner, preoccupation with job problems, these kinds of nighttime interferences lead to low-quality sex." If you're both constantly trying to make love at times when you're tired or anxious from a hurried day, when you've had too many Scotches or the children might peek in, then you ought to examine why you're pursuing this course of action. It may mean that you're really trying to avoid sex.

The best time to make love, according to the experts who are simply giving good common-sense advice, is when you're both relatively relaxed, have time to spare, and are assured of privacy.

WHERE

When I asked men and women about the "best" or "ideal" place to make love, the answers included:

"The best place was in a Los Angeles art gallery in the back behind some giant photorealist paintings. . . . Our son, conceived in that artistic way, is named after the gallery."

"I've always wanted to make love in a seedy motel. My husband-to-be took me to New Jersey to one of those truck-stop type places with flashing neon lights . . ."

"I dream of making love in a couchette on a Japan Airlines flight to Tokyo."

"Bed. You don't need fancy places. *You* provide the atmosphere. Also the bathroom floor—with an exercise mat underneath."

"My best experience was on top of an architect's drawing table. We had been discussing plans for a school playground . . ."

Sex manuals are divided on the subject of where to make love. Some say the only place to really explore and enjoy lovemaking is a comfortable bed with all the accoutrements nearby—candles, music, a glass of wine, fragrant sheets, etc. Other books extol the virtues of exotic places limited only by one's imagination, finances and physical fitness. As is often the case with such differing opinions and options, the wisest course to follow is your own inclination— wherever you both prefer is what works best for you.

THREE "SECRETS" OF GOOD SEX

Let each other know. Countless nuances of physical and emotional feeling occur when you make love. You must become sensitive to these changes by carefully reading your partner's physical responses and by revealing your specific reactions to various touches and movements. Simple phrases that begin with "I like that . . .," "More there . . .," "It feels so good when . . .," are not threatening or judgmental and give your partner a clear idea of what you need and want at differing times and under differing conditions.

Concentration. This is one of the great secrets to satisfactory lovemaking. All sorts of anxieties, fears and problems are likely to come right to bed with you; concentrating totally on what you are doing *moment by moment* is the best way to offset the kinds of insidious interferences that can slowly destroy even the best love relationship. Don't let your mind dwell on the office or the children's problems or what's going on next door or how your stomach looks. Both men and women told me thay can almost always tell if their partner is doing something by rote, and that's when the old love-killer—routine—starts to set in.

Giving and receiving pleasure. Many people with sexual problems suffer because they are judging themselves in terms of their performance or they're busy setting goals for themselves. ("I must achieve orgasm," "I must maintain my erection.") Refocusing on simply giving and receiving pleasure is one of the best ways of alleviating anxieties and opening yourselves up to the natural freedom and delight that are part of lovemaking.

MAGIC MOUNTAINS

> "There's kindergarten sex—that's what most people do—and then there's graduate school lovemaking. Now *that's* what you should write about!"

> "You hear that sex is oceanic, ecstatic, cosmic, volcanic. I think that's some kind of propaganda to keep poets in business. People who say those things are fooling themselves . . . or do they know something I don't know?"

I've found that most of the people I've interviewed fall into two camps: those who feel that making love is one of the most wonderful, sublime experiences a human can have, and those who secretly wonder what all the fuss is about. I suspect that the latter group never has learned the techniques that can heighten and intensify the physical and emotional aspects of making love.

In the '50s, Kinsey reported that the average time from penetration to ejaculation was three and a half minutes. If you ask people today how long they spend at making love a majority will usually say anywhere from twenty minutes to forty minutes. Asking indirect questions and researching statistics carefully, I found that most couples spend three to six minutes in actual physical intercourse with about three to ten minutes of touching and kissing before and usually less after. Those who speak of transcendent experiences usually spend *at least* half an hour to forty-five minutes making love.

Research has shown that *it may take a women twenty minutes or longer* to be fully aroused, whereas a man (under 50) usually becomes physically ready for orgasm in a much shorter period of time. It is lack of knowledge of this simple biological difference in timing between men and women that causes so many sexual problems. When women told me "I love my husband but I'm just not interested in sex anymore," it very often turned out to be a matter of their partners not stimulating them in the ways they needed in order to become sexually receptive. To put it into the plainest language: men must remember that most women take dramatically longer to be ready for intercourse and orgasm than they do. Not only must the majority of women be emotionally ready to make love, we must be physically ready through extended manual and oral stroking. "We would make love and I would feel I was just beginning to come to life when it was over. I was afraid to suggest doing it again," said one woman who echoes an all too common frustration.

"If men and women have such different timing mechanisms, how do we ever have good sex together?" asked one woman simply. The answer lies in what one very sexually active man I interviewed calls "Magic Mountains." Translated into understandable experience he's simply describing a sophisticated kind of lovemaking which consists of many peaks of pleasure for each partner over an extended period of time. The man is brought to the threshold or a peak of excitement (without ejaculation) one or more times and the woman is also brought to the threshold and crosses it (orgasm) once, or as many times as she desires (if she is multi-orgasmic). Within this extended lovemaking the couple may use any number of oral or manual techniques of stimulation or any sexual positions they may prefer. This kind of prolonged physical/emotional experience is a polar opposite to the biologically and emotionally insensitive "quickie" that many people admit is the staple of their sexual repertoire.

How, specifically, do you develop this kind of lovemaking? You need to be aware of certain kinds of control and letting-go, the very important differences in arousal patterns between you and your partner, the importance of certain techniques.

For men, much of the "secret" to extended

lovemaking involves the capacity to control ejaculation. At first this may seem difficult—it isn't. The key to success lies in recognizing the approach of the "point of no return" or what Masters and Johnson call the "stage of ejaculation inevitability." One man describes it as "that moment when you know that you are beginning to come but you can still hold yourself back. It's like knowing the point at which the wave is about to crest." It takes concentration to be sensitive to this phase and it may take you several experiences before you are completely aware of your own threshold.

You should also be totally aware of your responses to different types of thrusting. Deep, swift, direct thrusts lead more directly to ejaculation, whereas shallow, slanting, slow thrusts can help to retard it. As you begin to approach the point of no return, there are two things you may do to control ejaculation:

- Stop your movements for a moment or for as long as it takes for you to go back to a less aroused stage.
- You and your partner can use the squeeze technique.

If you stop for a few seconds or more you can go on to a new position where your thrusts are more shallow (e.g., your partner is on top, or side by side), or your partner can continue to give you an extraordinary sensation without overly stimulating you: she can take a small amount of saliva or lubricant and slowly circle the head of your penis with her fingers. She can also take your penis into her mouth and stroke the tip of it lightly with her tongue until you signal her that you would like to change to something else.

If you both decide to use the squeeze technique, here's how it works: Tell her when you are reaching the point of no return. She will then take her thumb and forefinger and encircle the top of your scrotum, making sure that the testicles are below the ring of her fingers. She gently squeezes or tightens her thumb and index finger together and at the same time applies a pressure toward your body with the back of her hand. Tell her what pressure works for you. The right amount of pressure and tightening for about six to ten seconds should effectively stop an ejaculation. However, if orgasm has begun, don't try to stop it. Be gentle, careful and cautious when using the squeeze technique—it may take several times before you can perfect it.

Note: If you have sex infrequently or have abstained for one reason or another, don't expect to have much control over ejaculation until you've made love once or several times.

In a sense women need the opposite of the control men must exercise. In order to experience orgasm(s), relaxation is crucial. Some women do accelerate orgasm by controlling and tightening their buttocks and thighs when they feel orgasm is imminent, but they do not seem to be a majority. Most women report that, as stimulation reaches a peak, they "give in" to the feelings and let orgasm "happen."

Perhaps the most important thing a woman can do

for her partner and for herself is to let him know how aroused she is. "The grope method is a highly inaccurate measure of where a woman is at sexually," says a knowledgeable man. "I can feel her nipples erect and I can sometimes tell exactly when the clitoris has retracted but I can still be way off. Sometimes women sigh or moan and it's not orgasm, it's just somewhere on the way to getting there. I'll say to a new lover, 'Give me directions, tell me to "keep on doing that" or "I need a few more minutes" . . .' and that's the best way I know to keep track of her special kind of timing."

POSITIONS

There are no "shoulds" or "musts" in lovemaking. When it comes to positions, each couple's particular physical and emotional makeup will dictate what feels best for them. In general, however, positions with the woman on top or astride give most intense stimulation to her, while allowing him greater control over ejaculation since his thrusting is not as direct. Many women are hesitant about being "on top" because they are embarrassed about their body image or they think a man might feel threatened. To the contrary, many men report this position as a favorite because it gives them a chance to lie back and enjoy visually and sensually—without being responsible for all the movements.

It may surprise you to know that until a generation ago, seventy percent of Americans had never tried any other position except old faithful, the so-called "missionary position." It's still preferred by many couples because it's unthreatening and gives face to face contact—and it just plain feels good. The missionary position can be used alone but is usually one of several positions and techniques used when a couple is involved with prolonged lovemaking as it is too easy for a man to come to orgasm because of the deep, direct thrusting involved. Variations of the man-on-top position allow for different depths of thrusting if a woman moves her pelvis in different ways. As a woman tilts her pelvis upward, lifts her legs higher, places her legs on a man's shoulders, or draws her knees to her chest, the thrusting becomes even deeper.

"The most effective coital position available to a man and a woman is the side-by-side or lateral position," according to Masters and Johnson. However, it doesn't seem to be the position of top choice for most of the couples that I interviewed. Masters and Johnson feel it is a democratic position and "there is no pinning of either the male or female partner. There is mutual freedom of pelvic movement in any direction and there will be no cramping of muscles or necessity for tiring support of body muscles." Perhaps it is the very democracy of the position that undermines it. "I've never been partial to side-by-side," is the way one knowledgeable woman put it. "I like switching between man-on-top and me-on-top, because it's sexier for each of us to be dominating some of the time."

Ancient and modern love manuals describe literally hundreds of sexual positions. You may feel emotionally or psychologically uncomfortable with some of them. "It reminds me of animals and homosexuals," said a secretary named Anne of the kneeling or "rear-entry" position. "I want to try anal sex with my fiancée," said one man, "but she says 'no' every time. It's the last holdout." If either of you would like to explore a new position or try something and your partner is negative or emotionally uncomfortable with it, ask (gently) why he or she feels that way. When Anne's lover explained that he found her extremely exciting in that position she was willing "to try it, just for a minute or two," which led her to the discovery that it was physically an exceptionally stimulating position for her as well.

Couples who enjoy an active, highly satisfying sexual relationship may use several positions or simply stick to two or three that they most prefer, occasionally experimenting with something new. Trying out too many different positions within one lovemaking session can be physically exhausting and usually adds up to nothing more than sexual athleticism. The fine art of extended lovemaking involves penetration in any of the different positions a couple may prefer, combined with techniques of manual and oral intercourse. Put more plainly, this means that you might start out with the woman astride, switch to oral sex for a while, then back to her on top, then back to oral or manual stimulation—or both—and then to the missionary position. This kind of lovemaking prefaced by kissing, hugging and erotic touching allows time for a woman to be thoroughly aroused and stimulated to orgasm(s) while her partner is being continuously

brought to peaks of pleasure before he finally
ejaculates.

A word here about simultaneous orgasm. Reactions
vary from "It's the best thing that can happen between
two people who love each other" to "I miss seeing all
the wonderful reactions my partner has if I'm having
an orgasm too." "It's an added treat but it's not
crucial" observes a man who sums up the majority
opinion.

ORAL SEX

Although many people talk about oral sex as a
taken-for-granted part of contemporary lovemaking,
it's an area still fraught with problems for both men
and women. Precisely because so many articles, books
and research experts say that "everyone" is doing it
and "everyone" should be enjoying it, there's a
reluctance in facing the reality of oral sex. The reality is
that many people have fears, conflicts and anxieties
about it.

Oral sex can be an exquisite part of making love, or
it can cause serious problems. Oral sex, as the words
imply, involves mouth/genital contact. By using oral
stimulation you don't rely on just the in-and-out
thrusting of penis and vagina to give each other
pleasure. With tongue, mouth and hands you can
create a whole new spectrum of sensations for each
other.

Oral sex can symbolize an acceptance and

acknowledgment of the deepest kind of physical intimacy between two people. If you're uncomfortable about oral sex—and many men and women are—learn as much about it as you can, and then take it one small step at a time, always keeping in mind that it is a very special way of giving pleasure.

One of the greatest areas of concern is body odors: the scents of men and women are natural attractants, but with so much emphasis on antisepticizing our environment, it's no wonder that we are afraid of our own scents. Several therapists that I talked with advised simply tasting your *own* scents in order to experience what your partner tastes and feels.

The most important aspects of oral sex are: giving pleasure to your partner, keeping in mind touch and timing, and sensitivity to your partner's degree of arousal.

For women: A lengthy section in *How to Make Love to a Man* was devoted to step-by-step oral sex and very many of the men and women I've spoken to since the book was published cited this as particularly helpful. For the purposes of clarity, these are the basic points repeated.

If you think of your mouth as the opening of a vagina and think of your hands as an extension of your mouth, you'll be able to use them to give the most pleasure. Begin by licking his penis with your tongue, keeping it well-lubricated with saliva. Make your tongue as sharp and pointed as you can and gently probe the areas around the most sensitive part, the head. If, at this point—or any other time—you begin to have thoughts that this is dirty or unpleasant or you are anxious, *concentrate totally* on what you are doing with your hands and mouth.

Now lick and stroke the penis, concentrating on the ridge that runs down the center of the underside. Keeping your tongue pointed, lightly flick it back and forth on the little ridge of skin where the head is joined to the shaft—for many men this is the most sensitive and responsive part of the penis. You may want to lick or kiss or stroke it lengthwise with your tongue. Remember to relax, remember to breathe, and focus on the fact that you are giving pleasure.

Now return to where the head and shaft connect. Take your time but don't hesitate: make smooth, fluid movements. You can envelop the penis with your mouth by keeping your lips drawn back in a tight oval covering your teeth and resting the penis on your tongue. The all-important oral friction now begins in which your mouth and tongue imitate the reciprocal motion and kneading action of the vagina. Move your mouth back and forth, up and down on the penis, constantly keeping in mind that your lips and mouth should feel like a very snug vagina. Begin slowly and increase your speed subtly at every forward stroke.

There seem to be two schools of thought about what is most pleasurable in oral sex. Some men contend that the more length taken into the mouth, the more satisfying it is to them. If your partner is in this group you might be interested to know that the trick Linda Lovelace used was to throw her head back off the edge of a bed so that her mouth formed one long passage. If you have a tendency to gag because he begins to thrust or your throat can't accommodate enough of his penis, take a second's pause, breathe deeply to relax your muscles, and continue on.

Another contingent of men feels that the head of the penis is the most sensitive area and the mouth need cover only that area plus one or two inches down the shaft. If your husband or lover is in this group, then use one of your hands as an extension of your mouth. Make a snug circle around the penis with your thumb and forefinger, keeping your lips in contact with your fingers. Now move your hand up and down the shaft of the penis in the same rhythm as your mouth. As your mouth goes down on the shaft, your hand moves downward too, and vice versa. You can also use your other hand to stroke the exposed base of the penis or use mild sensuous finger movements over the testicles and anal opening.

If you are in a position to see, you'll find that after a few minutes of this kind of intense stimulation the scrotum will begin to tighten and ascend toward the body cavity. This change means that orgasm is imminent. If you're not in a position to see, you'll probably know by his sighs or moans or tightening of leg muscles and toes. You can stop, switch to something else, or go on to a climax. If orgasm occurs you face the question of swallowing ejaculate. Don't do anything that you are uncomfortable with. Some men consider it a special love sign if a woman swallows their ejaculate. Others don't see it as "that big a deal," but it's really a matter of what you prefer to do.

Here are two "expert" suggestions that you may find helpful:

Applying a small amount of non-fragranced body lotion or K-Y Jelly to the penis makes your movements more fluid and provides the penis with even more friction. If you can't accept the slightly medicinal taste of lotions or gels, try applying lubricant to the lower shaft of the penis, the part that's in contact with your hand.

Several men said they are extremely stimulated by having the top of the scrotum encircled while oral sex is taking place. Use your free hand and join thumb and forefinger together in a circle around the top of the scrotum, just under the base of the penis. As you feel the scrotum tighten and rise with impending climax, relax your clasp or release your fingers altogether.

For men: Think of your tongue and hands as being able to give the most marvelous range of sensations to your wife or lover. Many women imagine that their lovers don't really like to stimulate them orally. She would be much reassured to hear you tell her "I love doing this with you," if that's what you honestly feel.

Remember that all your motions should be done continuously, unless your lover requests otherwise. Unlike a man's, a woman's level of arousal falls off steeply if stimulation is stopped even for a second or two. Some women respond quickly to oral/manual stimulation but many women need as much as ten to fifteen minutes—or more—to build up to a high peak of arousal.

You can use your tongue in many different ways: keep it pointed, then make it rounded or flat, and concentrate at first on the areas surrounding the clitoris, going from the "outer lips" of the vagina to the shaft of the clitoris and then to the clitoris itself unless you are signaled to stop (many women can take only very little direct stimulation). Move your tongue from right to left, from top to bottom, apply only *slightly* more pressure as you sense a higher degree of arousal. Do not worry if the clitoris is not yet "erect"; remember that a woman's arousal rate is much slower than yours. If at any time you begin to feel anxious or that you are not "doing the right thing for her," simply concentrate on your breathing and your tongue movements, and don't stop what you're doing. You might then switch to manually stimulating the clitoris (keeping your movements as sensitive and light as your tongue movements), while exploring the opening of the vagina with your tongue. Keep in mind that if your stimulation of the clitoris is too heavy-handed or your movements become too repetitive (for example, you continually stroke from left to right), you may cause the clitoris to go numb.

You can simulate the movement of your penis by thrusting your pointed or rounded tongue into the vaginal opening and then, if you wish, reverse this by stimulating the clitoris with your tongue and inserting a finger, or two, into the vagina, also simulating the in-and-out movements of your penis. (More than one woman reminded me to "please write that nails should be scrupulously clean and very short.") Some women like to be anally stimulated while oral sex is taking place. You can also apply a vibrator to the surface of the anus while you use your mouth and other hand to stimulate the clitoris/vagina. Keep in mind that the sensitive outer and inner vaginal area should be well lubricated with natural lubricants or K-Y Jelly or fragrance-free body lotion. Some men point out that the taste of gels or creams is unappealing. Experimenting with different brands to find one that is acceptable is well worth the trouble.

After a certain amount of stimulation, you may feel that you've "lost" the clitoris. What has happened is that it has retracted under its "hood," a natural response when a woman is highly stimulated or orgasm is about to occur. Continue your movements until orgasm. Unless she requests you to stop, go on stimulating her until she has another orgasm or switch to penetration or whatever you both prefer at the moment. Remember always that sexuality for a woman is not just genitally oriented. Remember to kiss her legs, arms, lips, breasts as your fingers continue to stimulate her.

AFTERWARD

About two-thirds of men and women go to sleep after the physical act of intercourse. Half of them nod off within minutes. But men and women who don't retreat into the privacy of their own dream worlds say that the time spent together after making love is invaluable in creating true intimacy. The key word here is *togetherness*: talking (*not* about business, the children, the mortgage), laughing, even watching TV or sharing a dish of ice cream with each other, extends warm, loving feelings into another realm of your lives. Let each other know by words or contact that you enjoyed yourselves, that your time together was important and meaningful.

If things haven't gone well, and there are obviously times when one of you will be under special stress or strain, don't dwell on the problem, but don't sweep it under the rug as if it didn't exist. Rather, reassure each other that you love each other, perhaps things weren't celestial tonight, but there's always tomorrow!

Two Valuable Ideas

Role-reversal was suggested earlier as an immediate and interesting way of finding out what kind of touch each of you prefers. It's just as fascinating and instructive—probably even more so—to try this with lovemaking itself.

Changing roles gives you a chance to show your husband or lover exactly how you would like to be made love to. If you can imagine that you are he, you can also gain some idea of what "performance anxiety" feels like for him and, if you are shy or usually passive, it becomes your responsibility to "take charge," to actually see what being the initiator feels like, and see how your partner responds to your movements. Conversely, role-reversal helps you to experience the timing and touching that your wife or lover needs and helps you to empathize with her emotional framework when you are making love.

Another practical idea that lets you both explore new kinds of experiences without feeling uneasy or anxious is "The Ten-Minute Agreement." You each agree to do what the other wants—for ten minutes. If you like, you can refine the "rules" by agreeing to exclude areas that make you very uncomfortable, or that you're not ready to explore. Proceed by telling your partner, for instance, that you'd like to try oral sex in a particular way, or you'd like to know what a new position or technique feels like. Alternate your requests so that each of you has two ten-minute spans to be pleasured in the way you would most like.

While this suggestion may sound overly clinical at first, you'll be quite surprised at the kinds of important information that can be exchanged when you have given each other permission to express your needs freely.

WHAT ABOUT BIRTH CONTROL?

The pill and intrauterine devices (IUD's) usually present no problems in lovemaking. Alternative methods that physically bar conception are known as barrier contraceptives. These include diaphragms, condoms and spermicides. Barrier contraceptives, when used correctly, are highly effective. The problem with them, however, is largely aesthetic.

You can tell we've come a long way sexually when the instruction pamphlet for a diaphragm suggests that your husband or lover may want to take part in inserting it. The point is: contraception is the responsibility of both of you and you need to talk about it openly. If you are shy or embarrassed, the chapter on "How to Talk About Sex" should help.

If you use a diaphragm or condom with spermicides, make sure you are using them correctly. Many people complain of the tastes of contraceptives. Washing the genital area gently and thoroughly after insertion usually eliminates the problem.

New contraceptives are being worked on continually. An exotic, but up until now still not widely known, tea is being explored as a simple, natural birth-control method; cervical caps are being reinvestigated and redesigned, and a new addition, which is in the final stages of evaluation, is "the sponge." The sponge, made of synthetic material, fits over the cervix and provides up to forty-eight hours of protection against pregnancy—it might be the ideal aesthetic contraceptive of the '80s.

Another area that couples may disagree on is intercourse during menstruation. Some people love it, others hate it, still others are lukewarm about it. The closest I could come to a consensus on the subject was that women who experience a heavy menstrual flow and/or cramps do not enjoy sex during the first day or two. (It's interesting to note that many women reported they are more desirous for sex on the three or four days preceding and following a menstrual period.) A gynecologist suggests that if you are uncomfortable about menstrual flow, insertion of a diaphragm will provide a temporary barrier. Instructions, by the way, usually point out that a diaphragm should be used *every* time a couple makes love.

ERECTION PROBLEMS

It can happen anytime, anyplace—to any man—and a one-time or some-times erection problem has an unpleasant way of escalating into something more serious unless it is dealt with right away.

No man is immune to the failure to attain an erection and the situation may occur for a large variety of reasons: too much stress, too much to drink, an unresponsive, indifferent partner—these are just a few possible causes. Keeping in mind that the trigger is usually a basic sexual fear, anxiety about performance, there's a great deal you can both do about the problem. In one form or another the "cure" involves taking your mind off of achieving an erection and simply getting yourselves to experience pleasure—not sex.

The first step to take is to talk about the situation.

One woman whose husband avoided lovemaking altogether after two episodes of impotence said, "I didn't want to say anything about it because I knew he felt miserable. I thought we'd just make love one night and it would go away. A year passed—with no sex at all—before we could bring ourselves to mention it." Don't fall into the common trap this couple set for themselves—talk about the situation as soon as it happens. Reassure each other that it's not earthshaking and that you love each other and resolve to deal with it together right away.

The wisest idea is to follow the advice that sex therapists give to patients. They suggest that couples do non-demanding sensuous stroking of each other's body excluding the genital areas. The next day touching and stroking the breasts and genitals is allowed—but no intercourse. After one or several sessions of this a man usually has a spontaneous erection.

Another suggestion that's commonly given is limiting yourselves to foreplay every other night for a week to ten days. Even if an erection occurs, intercourse does not take place until the week is over and emphasis should still be on pleasure and caring and sensual stimulation, not performance. Your attitude should be relaxed and casual: if I have an erection, fine, if not, there's always tomorrow.

If the situation has become chronic, it may not be a psychological problem but a physical one. Recent research shows that much of what was thought to be psychologically based impotence is physical in origin or may be due to certain medically prescribed drugs. Much can usually be done to help longstanding impotence of either type and you should talk with a sexual therapist or see your physician as soon as possible.

11
HOW TO BEAT
THE BEDROOM BLAHS

Sexual intimacy is only one part of true intimacy—
but it is crucial. If lovemaking tapers off into
obligation—or oblivion—a relationship is in serious
trouble. Talking at length with men and women from
East to West and North to South, I found that the
bedroom blahs most often set in after two to four years
of marriage. But it was not so unusual to hear of
instances where sexual intimacy broke down in as
short a period as three months.

The reasons for the onset of bedroom blahs are
complex and may include anger, insecurity,
resentment, anxiety about children or careers or
health, a growing apart emotionally, fear of sexuality,
fear even of pleasure—or just plain boredom. There

are several important ideas to keep in mind if a
relationship is to thrive year after year.

The first, and most important: *never take each other for
granted.* Be aware that a relationship or a marriage, like
every other vital thing, changes, and human beings
change, too. Recognizing emotional and physical
changes and changing needs is a way of growing
together instead of growing apart. Most experts agree
that one of the major reasons for the breakdown of a
marriage is unmet needs. A wife may need more
affection, more nurturing, a more understanding
listener; a husband may need mothering or more
frequent lovemaking—the list of needs is almost
endless and is, of course, different for each of us. In
order to avoid the anxiety of confronting our partners,
many of us—consciously or not—hide what we truly
want or need. This sets off a nasty chain reaction: if
you don't say what you want you not only won't get it
but you will probably also experience resentment,
anxiety, anger, hostility, depression or guilt. Making
your needs and desires clear is *absolutely essential* if a
relationship is to survive—let alone thrive.
Furthermore, these needs change as we outgrow our
own beliefs and attitudes and self-images. A
continuing dialogue over the years is the only way that
these changes will be recognized and dealt with. This
holds true in all aspects of intimacy as well as in the
sexual realm.

A love relationship is entered into by *two* people.
Boredom and bickering can quickly replace excitement
and fascination if two people do not grow separately as
well as together. When you nourish your independent

whole self you can allow that self to merge with another. Self-esteem and a sense of worth that is renewed and cultivated over the years is an essential element in a long-lasting relationship.

Preserving the emotional status quo is another insidious trap that many of us fall into. Rather than saying or doing anything that will rock the relationship, many men and women hold on to patterns that are routine and boring. Lovemaking, vacations, dinner-table conversation become predictable, unprovocative and antiseptic. If you think you're "pleasing your partner" by not saying what you want or feel—or saying what you think he or she wants to hear—you're making a major mistake.

One good way to identify this trap is to check how often you say to yourself, "I should," I must," "I ought to," "I wish I could." If you find these phrases overly familiar, you need to thoroughly examine your own needs as well as the foundations of your relationship.

One more aspect of a long-lasting love relationship needs special mention. You are not going to have a transcendent experience every time you make love. If you feel that the fireworks should go off every time, you're both going to have to fake a lot. And faking is precisely the opposite of what intimacy is all about. Sexual desire, sexual passion, and sexual enthusiasm, like other emotions, ebb and flow. Even in the closest, most intense relationships, lovemaking will have its ups and downs. This is natural, normal and healthy, but what *should* always last is the commitment to making the relationship work.

Either of you may not feel like making love when the other does. It's perfectly normal to be on differing sexual wavelengths. Each of us has a differing level of sexual drive and this level probably changes daily. If you've established good communication, you should be able to express what it is you do or don't want without hurting the other person. If you're not interested in sex at the moment, it's helpful to try and explain why you feel the way you do. Worries at the office, anxiety about money, health, career and family can all cause a temporary lack of desire.

If you have no special problems and still are just not in the mood to make love, it may simply be the normal ebb and flow of sexual desire. But be honest with yourself and each other. Don't say it's the mortgage payments that are troubling you when you really are angry about your mother-in-law or what your partner said to you at dinner last week. Often when you express what you're upset about, the sexual barricades open up and you can make love without any negative emotional baggage getting in the way. However, if you find that the lack of desire continues for more than ten days or so it's a wise idea to first see if a physical problem exists and then, if necessary, consult a sexual therapist.

Before we get down to the specifics of beating the bedroom blahs, there's one more important thought to keep in mind: the *"seductiveness of loving."* By this I mean that a person who feels truly loved, who feels that he or she is the sole focus of attention, who feels that his or her lover is truly carried away by desire, that person is surely a candidate for long-lasting happiness.

The following lists "For Her" and "For Him" give some information that each of you might find useful in keeping things on an exciting, romantic, sensuous level year after year . . .

FOR HER

Let him know that you are truly interested in sex. Most of the men that I interviewed said they felt their wives or girlfriends were "lukewarm," "too uptight" or "too inhibited" about sex. Being truly interested means completely and totally enjoying your own natural, healthy, lustful sexuality. For one woman this might mean allowing herself to experience the pure physicality of "having sex" or recognizing her impulses for lovemaking instead of subduing them or feeling guilty. For another it might mean something as simple as letting her husband know that she isn't wearing anything except a lace garterbelt and stockings under her discreet black cocktail dress. For still another, it might mean summoning the courage to have a frank discussion of the sexual problems in the marriage or allowing herself to explore sexual fantasies with her husband.

Letting him know that you truly feel sex is great and that you look forward to it with an open mind and a willing body is one of the greatest turn-ons any man can have.

How to Make Love to Each Other

Sending sensuous signals. "Clothes," says Alison Lurie in an article on "Sex and Fashion" (*New York Review of Books,* October 22, 1981), "can tell us whether people are interested in sex. . . . Soft, flowing, warm-hued clothes traditionally suggest a warm, informal, affectionate personality and the garment which is partially unfastened not only reveals more flesh but implies that total nakedness will be easily achieved. Tight, bundled-up or buttoned-up clothes (if not figure-revealing) are felt to contain a tight, erotically held-in person."

If to the outside world you must be a buttoned-up, business-suited lawyer or a conservatively dressed mother or efficient office manager, you can send a sensuous message to your husband by wearing clothes that he can respond to in the private times you have together. Lacy, revealing black underwear and stockings are traditionally considered erotic and many men are instantly stimulated by seeing a woman thus arrayed. But caution applies here. If you're the type of woman who has never worn especially sexy underthings, *warn* your husband beforehand that you're thinking of trying something new. He may be bewildered by your style or he may even be turned off by it.

Speaking of style, stick to clothes that you feel comfortable wearing. "I'd feel totally out of character in baby dolls," reports a Los Angeles secretary that I interviewed, "and my discomfort would certainly show. I like pajamas. Recently I changed from flannel to satin ones and my husband finds them very seductive. If you *feel* sexy in it, you'll *be* sexy in it."

"There's a difference between sexy and blatant in

clothes,'' says a tall, courtly Atlanta hotel owner, who sums up the way a great many men feel. ''If something is too tight or too clingy, I get embarrassed, but I like the way a woman looks in silky fabrics and sheer stockings and dresses that let me know she has a body underneath. If that makes me a male chauvinist pig, so be it!''

Visual effects. Why is it men find black underwear so sexy anyway? Because, to the beholder's eyes, black lacy stuff immediately implies a certain eroticism and perhaps even a delightful wickedness in its wearer. The underwear itself isn't sexy, it's the way a man *sees* a woman who's wearing it that's the turn-on.

As more research pinpoints the effects of early visual responses in males, it seems logical that women might use this information as an aid in lovemaking. The sight of black stockings or a garterbelt flung over a bedroom chair, pictures in an erotic photography book, explicit drawings in sex shop catalogs or miniature erotic Indian or Persian prints—all of these can evoke powerful physical responses from men and elicit appreciation for the woman who understands their importance.

In recent years, some couples have discovered that they are turned on by taking Polaroid pictures of each other when they are making love. One husband and wife whom I interviewed took pictures of themselves together by cleverly moving mirrors around in their bedroom. The same idea of visual stimulation applies here: seeing different positions and different parts of the body can be a powerful aphrodisiac for both men and women.

Another way of exploring the visual world is to

make up word-pictures. "The mind is the most important sexual instrument we have," someone once remarked. One woman I interviewed told me that she and her husband exchange erotic stories, lingering over the most delicate and explicit details to produce an almost photographic, highly erotic imprint on their minds. If your imagination isn't up to storytelling, try reading aloud to each other from erotic books. The *Kama Sutra* and Ovid's *Ars Amatoria* are two wonderful works that are available in most libraries and bookstores.

FOR HIM

Romance, romance, romance, romance. Hardly enough can be said to emphasize the importance of romance and, indeed, most women would say it's critical if you want to keep your marriage exciting and alive. Romance means being spontaneous, adventurous, exciting, Prince Charming. Romance means bringing home a rose or a bunch of violets for no other reason than to say "I love you" or giving your wife or lover a record or tape of music you both feel is very special.

For many women romance seems to mean *doing* something, not just saying something. "Sometimes it can be just too easy to repeat 'I love you.' It meant much more when my lover gave me Shakespeare's love sonnets with a wonderful inscription," says a Delaware computer programmer. Sending a card or a note with a poem or an endearing phrase does more to woo her and keep her happy than a string of routine verbal endearments. A friend told me of a journalist who took this concept to what may be its ultimate: Ed, a foreign correspondent, was always traveling and was away from his lover, Jan, for much of the time. One morning, while in the bathroom, Jan unraveled the toilet paper to find small white slips of paper saying "I love you," "I miss you," "I shall return . . ." fluttering out of the roll.

What seems to turn women off most is goal-oriented or rote romance. "You can instinctively tell if he's sending flowers or taking you to a special dinner so he can get your clothes off sooner," says one woman. When the "goal" of romance is simply to be romantic, you'll very often end up making love.

Understanding. Take time to really *listen* to what she is saying and try to understand what her attitudes and problems are and how they are different from yours. If she says she is tired, she probably really means it. Nothing would seduce a woman more than offering to run a bath for her or to make her a comforting hot toddy if she's exhausted from ten hours with the children and/or a desk full of problems. If you take the time out to empathize with her, to find out what *her* day has been like, she'll be more grateful—and more loving—than you might imagine.

Talk to her. "Nothing is more frustrating than a man who holds back his feelings," says a Nashville secretary, and her words are echoed by many women. The man who makes an effort to communicate what's going on in his inner and outer life is much cherished.

The man who simply takes time to talk to his wife or lover is showing her that he really cares, that he really wants their relationship to flourish and endure.

Talking to her also means telling her that you love her and you think she is the most beautiful, charming, interesting, woman in the world—*if you mean it.* And don't feel that if you've told her once that her sense of humor is sensational, that she's a terrific mother or she's a brilliant hostess that she can live on that for the next twelve months. We need to hear that we're valuable, needed and loved—and we need to hear it often. Most of all, tell your wife or lover how much you really desire her—in bed and out of bed. There is simply no greater turn-on than that. "Tell her she's a wonderful lover and she'll become one," says a smart and sexy Portland man. "Women need to feel safe and secure and attractive. A man who tells his wife he's longing to make love to her will find her leading him straight to the bedroom."

If you remember that baby girls are highly sensitive to sounds and voices, you can see why grown-up females are charmed, delighted and highly responsive to the lover who reads poetry to them. The classic things great lovers do—like sharing poetry or whispering love-words—have kept romance alive and thriving century after century . . .

Take charge. A woman who spends her time taking care of the children and you, plus working at the office, needs to be taken care of too. "The best thing Joe ever did was give me a complete weekend where I had nothing to do but feel like a princess," said one woman I interviewed. "He'd planned it down to the last detail. Bought tickets for a Broadway play, made reservations at an elegant restaurant, there was even a bottle of wine chilling at the table as we sat down. When we got home I found a locket on a gold chain hidden under my pillow, and the next morning I was treated to breakfast in bed with the dishes done too . . . I'm already thinking up some very special treats for him."

You may not be able to take the Prince Charming role quite so far, but think of telling her: "Circle the calendar for Saturday night and expect to be surprised!" Buy tickets for a special concert, or plan a lazy brunch at a favorite restaurant or organize a romantic picnic under the stars with a brown paper bag filled with bread and wine and cheese. Tuck in a small present (her favorite cologne, a book, a card, a bouquet of flowers) as a lovely finishing touch.

12
BARING YOUR SOULS:
When, Where and How to
Talk About Sex

Merrily is an energetic, articulate, red-headed woman of 31 who has been married to Doug, 34, for nine years. They live in a charmingly restored townhouse in Philadelphia where they share many interests, including a passion for gourmet cooking and rare, exotic orchids which they nurture in a small but beautifully efficient greenhouse that Doug and their two young sons have built together.

Scratch the surface of what the neighbors would tell you is an idyllic relationship and, on an intimate level, you'll find that Merrily has been faking orgasm for years; she is too frightened to ask for the lengthy stimulation that she needs in order to fully enjoy sex.

She feels ashamed and guilty that she wants more—a lot more—and believes that it's too late to say anything about The Problem, even if she could muster the courage to talk to Doug. In a very deep place she feels her husband would be devastated—perhaps even leave her—if he were to find out the truth, so she concentrates on "all the good things" that fill up her marriage. Sex is not so important after all, is what she keeps telling herself.

Doug is a quiet, stable man who isn't given to expressing his feelings often, yet over the past years he has increasingly had one-time sex with call girls who are easily available to him in the hotels that he stays in when traveling for his engineering business. Doug doesn't think about his "dates" and has told himself time and time again that his lovemaking with Merrily is "what naturally happens after you've been married for nine years." He can live without the kind of sex he wishes he could have with Merrily as long as she is happy—and she certainly seems to be. She responds quickly to him, he hears her small sighs of delight almost as soon as she is in his arms, but it would be nice to try something that he would especially like once in while . . .

Merrily and Doug's marriage—or half-marriage—is, sadly, very typical. Sexual researchers have estimated that at least fifty percent of marriages suffer from sexual problems, but I would put the figure even higher.

An intelligent management consultant I interviewed told me the following:

"Judd and I were married for six years. Sex was

128

good but had never been great. In the last three years
we made love about six or eight times, a few other
times he was impotent. My diaphragm was so old and
unused it began to look like a piece of lace. I didn't talk
to him about it because he is a very private person and
I thought it would make him anxious, perhaps even
totally impotent. I know sex is a very delicate subject
for a man and I wanted to protect Judd from feeling
that I was making demands. I kept thinking things
would improve if we had less stress in our lives, if we
took a vacation, if we moved to a nicer apartment . . . I
fell into an affair and finally turned to a therapist for
help . . . I now realize that by 'protecting' Judd from
what I thought was his problem, I myself wasn't facing
the problem either. I'm not sure now whether our
marriage will survive. I feel three years of both our
lives have been wasted."

This story too is a sadly common one: a sexual
problem crops up and becomes magnified as it is
neglected and pushed aside. If Judd and his wife could
have faced the situation together in the early stages,
much of the depression, anger, guilt and resentment
which they both feel, would have been avoided. It's
almost axiomatic to say that the longer a problem exists
the harder it may be to tackle, but the prognosis in the
sexual area is encouraging: sexual difficulties can
respond remarkably to open discussion and a
willingness to work on them. One marriage counselor
put it this way, "If you can accept a problem, you can
usually solve it."

Merrily's faking of orgasm, her husband's unspoken
needs, Judd's erection problems, *can* be dealt with.

Merrily's first step would be to see a gynecologist for a physical exam to determine if there are any physical causes (tipped uterus, unusual placement of clitoris, etc.) that might be interfering with orgasm. Just discussing the problem with a physician should help to ease some of her anxieties and make her realize that she's not unusual—and that she can *talk* about it. Since The Problem has existed for so many years it would be wise not to blurt out to Doug "I've been faking." It would be more productive to suggest to him that there are areas in their physical relationship that might need some updating or reevaluation. As an opening to a discussion, she could say, "I've read an article in a magazine (or a book or I've heard a radio talk show) on some sexual problems and I was wondering if you are satisfied with our lovemaking . . ." Similarly, Judd and his lover have to face their difficulties—in this case erection problems—but before any physical steps can be taken, the situation needs to be acknowledged and talked about. The rest of this chapter tells exactly how to do that.

Perhaps the most important tool we have in sustaining a healthy marriage is communication—a much overused but critically important word. Without communication a relationship is not likely to flourish, much less survive. "You can have a 'nice' marriage where there are no conflicts or problems," says a sage marriage counselor, "but a good marriage is one in which problems are faced, discussed, and dealt with." If you can express what you really need and want without fear or shame, your desires are often met with surprising quickness. When fears of failure and humiliation and rejection are expressed openly, they lose their power to hurt. "I am afraid you'll leave me if I say what I really want . . ." "I'm afraid that I can't maintain my erection" or "I feel vulnerable and exposed when I do that . . ." are surprisingly often countered with "I want us to stay together, and I'll give it all the effort I can" or, even more commonly, "I didn't know you felt that way. Tell me more . . ."

Unless you tell your partner how you feel and what you want, how is he or she to know? One of the greatest problems in communication between two people lies in the assumption that your partner *automatically senses* what you want or don't want. Almost nothing could be further from the truth. "Trying to be an effective lover for oneself and one's partner without communication," says Dr. Kaplan, "is like trying to learn target shooting blindfolded." Masters and Johnson and the rest of the experts would wholeheartedly agree.

WHERE, WHEN AND HOW

Once again there are no "musts" or "shoulds" in communicating with each other, but a few guidelines can help in the learning process. *When* is the best time to talk about a sexual problem or a sexual need? "As soon as possible" is the obvious answer, although it may not be so obvious to many couples. Talk about a problem when you feel it brewing, but no time is ever too late if the subject is handled intelligently and sensitively. If you feel overwhelmed or incapable of broaching the subject at all, it would be wise to seek the counsel of a well-qualified therapist or to first talk the situation over with a clergyman or your physician.

Where is the best place to talk? Anywhere that is private, where you will not be interrupted, and can have an open-ended amount of time, will make communication much easier. Bed is usually *not* a good place to discuss problems as it seems to put many people on the defensive. Some couples I talked with find that sitting around the kitchen table with a cup of coffee or tea is "neutral" yet intimate and comfortable territory.

Where or when to talk about sex are relatively minor matters—the biggest problem for most people is *how*.

The first step is something you do alone. Be honest with yourself about your own needs. Investigate what you *really* want and feel, what you like and don't like. Assess your emotional state: are you angry, depressed, frustrated, have you been settling for less than you really want? Many people neglect or avoid their own responses for so long that they're not even aware of how they feel. Being fidgety, irritable or tense can be another way of expressing deeper, more hidden feelings that you may be afraid to acknowledge. Tears, for example, may actually represent rage or resentment for many women who do not allow themselves to be directly angry. The following story, told to me by a young banking executive, is a fairly typical example of the way you can hide your own feelings from yourself:

"I love flowers and my husband knows this," she
said with a sad smile, "I always justified his never
bringing me any by saying that he was too busy or he
just wasn't the type to go into a florist's—whatever
that 'type' might have been! I share an office with a
woman whose lover recently sent her a beautiful
spring bouquet and I started to cry when I saw it. I was
so surprised at my tears and even more amazed when
I thought it over and realized that an enormous feeling
of anger was welling up against my husband for never
paying attention to something I really loved . . . for
never paying attention to *me*."

Once you're aware of how you really feel and what
you really want—or don't want—you're ready to
begin a discussion with your partner, but remember
that despite all the emphasis given to talking about
your feelings, it's usually not a good idea to just dump
them on your mate. Saying "I feel this," or "I feel
that" may not be productive unless you can say *why*
you feel that way. When you give your partner the
reason you like or don't like something you can go on
to a two-way discussion of the specifics of the problem
rather than a confrontation or a fight about why you're
doing, or refusing to do, something.

Try expressing a problem this way:

"I don't like oral sex because I don't know how to do
it," or "I'm anxious about oral sex because I have the
idea that it is dirty," or "I'm uncomfortable about the
way my body might taste or smell to you," or "I don't
like doing that because I feel so vulnerable," or "I'm

133

anxious about exploring fantasies because I'm afraid I'll do something that will embarrass me," or "I'm worried about performing because it's so important."

If you're asking for something that you need or would like more of, try phrasing it in a positive way rather than a demanding one:

"I love it when you take a lot of time to kiss me . . ."

"I enjoy a lot of touching and stroking there . . ."

"I feel great when you suck at my breasts . . ."

"I wonder how you feel about exploring fantasies . . ."

"I love feeling your mouth on my penis . . ."

A 29-year-old teacher from Boston summed this idea up clearly when she said, "It's amazing how often you get what you want if you ask for it in the right way."

Once you've started to say what you need and want, ask your partner what he or she feels. The idea is to get a two-way discussion going. "What's going through your mind when I ask about . . ?" "How do you feel about that?" are good ways to begin. Therapists remind couples not to feel defensive but rather to empathize with each other in talking things out. It's important for you to see the other side, so, even though it may be difficult, make a special effort to feel what your partner is feeling—rejection, insecurity, anxiety, anger—and you'll find it much easier to understand the problem and begin to resolve it.

Even though you've just read through all of the above you still may feel anxious about broaching the subject of sex. You're in the majority. Most of the people I spoke with say it's hard to talk about sexuality, especially if you've had a relationship over a period of years where the subject has been carefully avoided or considered off-limits altogether.

Before I started doing interviews on sexuality I realized I was anxious about talking to people on such an intimate subject. My first meeting was with a man named Mike who spoke in a pleasant, even voice without a trace of hesitation or embarrassment about the most intimate experiences he'd had with an astonishing number of women. For him, sexuality and making love were as natural as the air he breathed. As he talked I found myself feeling much less uptight, although I don't think I once looked up from my notepad during the hour we were together.

It was only after a number of interviews that I realized that Mike's way of talking about sexuality was a key to defusing anxieties—mine and other people's. His comfortable, casual, and above all non-judgmental, non-defensive style was infectious, which simply means that if you learn to talk openly and naturally about sex it's very likely that the person you're talking with will respond in an equally relaxed and open way and you'll have a more honest, productive discussion.

If, no matter how you try to relax, you find you're still hesitant to talk about sex or to even bring up the subject, you might try using a method that the behaviorists say yields a high success rate. Practice an imaginary conversation with your partner, using phrases such as the ones above ("I like it when you . . .", "I'm anxious about this because . . .", etc.).

Imagine further that your husband/wife empathizes with your comments and feelings and responds warmly to what you are saying, revealing desires and needs and joys of his/her own. Go on imagining and play out the whole discussion, keeping each of your responses in a positive, enlightening tone. The therapeutic idea behind this imaginary exercise is that if a situation is practiced in advance with a *positive* outcome, the chances of its turning out that way in reality will be greatly increased.

One of the most positive steps you can take in working out communication difficulties is to resolve to work on the problems *together*. Acknowledge to each other that you might feel uncomfortable or embarrassed and then resolve that you *both* share the responsibility for openly saying what it is that you want and need from each other. Once you both agree to share the responsibility for your lovemaking you may well find that it begins to improve in an amazingly short period of time.

A postscript: Quite a number of women have told me that shared responsibility for communication exists only in the minds of therapists and marriage counselors. "Once again the woman is really the one who has to do all the work," is the way a suburban housewife states it. "We have to tiptoe around the male psyche and usually it's the woman who is forced to bring up the problems." In the best of all possible worlds, each partner should take equal responsibility for keeping the lines of communication open, but in our world men have been programmed to be strong and silent and they often find it impossibly difficult to express what they feel or what they need. *Someone* has to take the initiative to communicate so that a relationship can grow and perhaps, at this stage in our emotional evolution, women are better equipped to take the lead.

13

LOVE NEGOTIATIONS

He wants to have sex every night. She wants to make love three mornings a week. Is it resolvable?

Oral sex—what he needs is what's hardest for her to give. Can they both feel comfortable and be satisfied?

She wants a monogamous marriage. He loves her but cannot promise he'll be faithful. What can they do about it?

WHY LOVE DOESN'T CONQUER ALL

A problem like the very common ones mentioned above is likely to crop up anytime in a relationship— what do you do?

There are three basic ways of coping: ignoring and

avoiding the difficulty, letting resentment or fear or anger build up over a period of time until the lid blows off (but nothing gets resolved from the fireworks) or facing the problem squarely, talking about it, and negotiating a solution.

Why do so many people balk at the idea of "negotiating" a settlement to an intimacy problem or a sexual standoff? "It's because we're told that love will find a way," says a matrimonial lawyer in New York, who adds, "If love could find a way there'd be no divorce courts." What love does when it comes to solving a problem or healing a rift is to give each person the patience, the determination and the desire to go on despite the pain, the anxieties, and the exposure that may be involved in negotiating a resolution. In other words, it is love that makes you want to be together and to make the changes that will keep you together.

I think there's another reason why people balk at the idea of negotiating, and that's because they really don't know how to negotiate. Many "experts" told me that negotiation is an art. "You have to have a handle on interpersonal transactions and an almost psychic sense of timing," said one Wall Street executive who negotiates multi-million-dollar deals with unnerving alacrity. However, in talking to skilled negotiators—businessmen, divorce lawyers, transactional therapists, etc.—I've found that the "art" of negotiating, specifically in intimate matters, is not some inaccessible esoteric activity but one that can be easily learned and practiced with immediate results. In the exceptionally delicate areas of love and sex, negotiation can be a direct, non-threatening means to effecting real, meaningful and long-lasting changes in a relationship.

YOU-ME-US:
A NEW WAY OF SEEING YOUR RELATIONSHIP

The ground rules or guidelines of loving negotiations include, first, visualizing an equal triangle where you are at one point, your partner at another, and "the relationship" at the third point. Two of you are going to negotiate, keeping in mind that not only each of you but the third entity, your relationship, will gain from your dealings together.

Perhaps the most important aspect of negotiation is that all three of you "win" or, to put it conversely, no one loses. "When I sit down to do a deal," says a well-known Hollywood agent, "I want my client as well as the movie studio or producer to feel that they've each gotten something. If one side feels they've been taken, it's not a good deal and I've learned from long experience that a slew of problems will inevitably crop up. If you negotiate a contract where both sides feel comfortable, the future-problem factor is almost sure to be zero. I sit down with the parties and say 'We all want something. We're here to work something out so that we are all satisfied.'" Expert negotiators agree with him on every point.

The second idea to remember is that you and your partner are *equals.* Each of you has equal time, equal responsibility and equal importance in the relationship and each of you respects the other and what he or she has to say.

Now comes the pre-negotiating part. Assuming that you both have acknowledged a specific problem (for example, each of you has different ideas on sexual frequency, oral sex, fantasy sex), begin by asking yourselves these questions:

What is it that I really want?
What sort of compromise can I live with comfortably?
What would really be unacceptable?

Don't censor yourself in any way. What you *really* want may be totally irrational or illogical, but lay it out on the table to yourself so that you can answer the questions honestly. Now, assuming that the negotiation is to be on a sexual aspect of your relationship, you might go through a process like this:

What I really want is to _____ *every* time we make love.

I can live with having _____ only some of the times we make love but I would prefer it to occur the majority of times we make love.

I would be most unhappy if there were no _____ in our marriage.

Be totally truthful with yourself. Unless each of you first works your way through the complete thinking-out process you won't be able to negotiate fairly for yourselves.

The next step is to start a discussion about the problem. Keeping in mind the thoughts in the previous chapter, either of you might initiate a conversation by saying:

> "I want to tell you that I feel anxious about _____ because . . ."

> or

> "I know it's been hard for us to be open about sex but I'd like to know what you think about _____."

> or

> "I think it's important for us to talk about _____ because I feel anxious (unhappy, fearful, uptight, etc.) . . ."

As you were totally honest with yourself in assessing what you want, you must now be totally honest with your partner in saying what you want—or don't want, what would give you the most pleasure, what gives you the least, what you can live with, what you absolutely can't take. "Many women have a tendency to compromise before they ever say a word," warns a therapist. "For example, she may want total monogamy *no matter what,* but she says to her husband, 'It's okay to have a one-night stand if you're on a business trip.'" This pre-compromising is detrimental in two ways. Her husband doesn't know what she really wants or that she has already compromised in advance without his knowledge. Since he has no way of knowing what she has already "given" him, she's bound to be resentful of any final settlement where she must compromise even further.

Each of you should say—not demand—what he or she wants, no matter how unreasonable, and know that the other person won't ridicule or leave. "Desires are desires," says one psychologist. "It's unwise and dangerous to deny or ignore them." You may secretly wish to make love to sitar music sitting in a rocking chair at the stroke of midnight and be too embarrassed to admit it. However, if you tell your husband or wife this is something that is important to you, you may find that your partner will accommodate you more often than you might have dared hope, especially if you make a reciprocal offer of something that he or she has been longing for.

Negotiating begins when you've both honestly stated your needs and you start the back and forth discussion of working out a settlement. Listen—really listen—to what each of you has to say. Don't be thinking of what *you're* going to say next while the other person is talking. Try to empathize and understand what it is that your husband or wife wants and why he or she wants it. Listen carefully but *stay on your side*—don't jump to his or her point of view to please or placate. Too often one partner (again usually the woman) will say, "You're right, that's silly of me," or "I really don't know what I want," when she's afraid to tell the truth for fear of rejection. Men and women have different needs and expectations in lovemaking, so keep these in mind without sacrificing your own point of view.

Deal with one problem at a time. If you're talking

about oral sex or the need for fantasy, don't bring in the children or your parents or the neighbors' "sexual swinging" or anything else. Stick to the specific area that you are confronting so that you can make changes there; don't throw in statements or accusations like "but who brings home the biggest paycheck"—that's another subject and should be dealt with at another time.

Let's examine the three problem areas described at the beginning of this chapter.

Jim wants to have sex every night. Sarah wants to make love three mornings a week. In one form or another this is one of the most common problems known to marriage. Differing sex drives, whether they stem from inborn or cultural or male/female differences, can cause major problems. How to resolve? First both of you must talk about your specific needs, making clear what "sex" means and what "making love" means to each of you. Then describe why you feel the way you do. "I'm too tired at night . . .," "I'm afraid the children will hear . . .," "I'm not really getting satisfied because I need more sex, more physical contact." When each person really hears the other person's needs, and *wants* the relationship to continue, then meaningful changes can be made. A frank discussion of how and where and when a couple can realistically make love, given their differing physical needs and the demands that children and careers make on both, leads to negotiation and comfortable compromise. Jim and Sarah solved the problem by agreeing to "rapid" sex two or three nights a week and leisurely lovemaking on Saturday or Sunday mornings when the kids were engrossed in TV. For another couple a resolution could involve another kind of lovemaking pattern or scheduling a romantic weekend away from home once a month with more "quick" sex during the week.

Oral sex—what Jonathan needs is what's hardest for Amy to give. Another sensitive area of enormous misunderstanding is oral sex—for both men and women. The first step is acknowledging the existence of the difficulty: for example, Jonathan has told Amy that he "really needs" oral sex but is not getting enough of it. If unlike Jonathan you can't express your needs so directly, you might begin by saying, "There's something I need to discuss with you and it may be difficult for us both. . . ." The situation, of course, might as easily be reversed, and Amy would be the one who is needing more oral or manual stimulation. A discussion of why oral sex is so difficult for Amy (her strict religious background, guilt, resentment, her fear of ejaculate, etc.) and why it is so important to Jonathan (most intimate act for him, symbolizes giving and caring, etc.) yields valuable insights for both of them. Amy promises to research books with information on sexual techniques and agrees to "try it for a few times." If the problem still exists, she and Jonathan agree that they will both seek the help of a therapist. A negotiated resolution for another couple with a similar problem might be as simple as having her not take ejaculate into her mouth.

Lynn wants a monogamous marriage. Paul loves her but cannot promise he'll be faithful. When Paul says that he is not able to promise fidelity and Lynn has expressed a need for total monogamy, they've already taken step one in negotiation and openly faced what they each want and feel. Paul is a highly sexual man who takes two long sales trips a year for his company. He doesn't want to "cheat" on Lynn but he says masturbation does not satisfy his sexual needs. The negotiated solution: Lynn will accompany him on one trip a year and he will come home for one weekend during his other trip. Should she choose not to travel with him he would be "free" to seek sexual relief but only from an impersonal one-time encounter.

Lynn and Paul's settlement or contract was worked out over many months of negotiations. "At first we were frightened to talk about it. I felt he was totally unreasonable and he felt I was wildly unrealistic, but we kept going back again and again to see what alternatives and options would make us both feel comfortable. What we finally agreed on was something that was workable for each of us and kept the relationship going. The solution may sound clinical, but knowing exactly what our boundaries were gave us enormous relief," says Lynn.

Some negotiations will be relatively simple and some will be complex, taking days or weeks or even months to achieve as new solutions and new ideas are offered and thought over by both parties.

If you come to a complete impasse, agree together to see a therapist or counselor who may be able to offer new insights and suggestions. Remember, too, that what you settle on isn't engraved in stone. You may find, after a period of time, that you're unhappy with the negotiated "deal" and you want to change it. The process then begins all over again: "I feel I'd like to make some changes about—," or "I'd like to update our agreement. . . ." Facing changes and growth and embracing the freedom to ask for what you want is what makes a relationship thrive, deepen and last.

14
FANTASY:
How Far Is Too Far?

Whips, chains, black-leather masks and other malevolent-sounding items often come to mind when you say "sexual fantasy." Many people automatically shun sexual fantasies as "kinky" or "bad," yet exploring and acting out fantasies can be helpful as well as exciting in a relationship. "Sharing unknown, imaginative worlds can add a marvelous dimension and new insights to the intimate life of two people," states a respected New York marriage counselor who often suggests to couples that they begin to explore the fascinating world of fantasy as a form of therapy.

What happens when you delve into your imagination—and your partner's? "You might uncover a secret, hidden self and that makes two people who are close, even closer," says Jennifer, a fashion

149

coordinator for a Midwestern department store chain.
Jennifer and her husband, Matthew, discovered that
she had a "dominating, aggressive, wild side" when
they began to verbally exchange fantasies after several
years of marriage. "It really turns me on when she tells
me the incredible ways she's going to do it to me,"
says her husband.

The risk-taking involved in baring parts of our most
private selves can also intensify and deepen intimacy,
and therapists point out that verbalizing your fantasies
or sharing your special worlds with each other also
helps provide an escape from rigid, inhibiting,
"uptight" roles. Most important of all, fantasy can help
many men and women to begin to communicate real
needs, desires and wishes in a non-threatening way.

Fantasy can, and should be, fun. Those couples who
enjoy acting out or talking about their fantasies very
often report a special, exhilarating sense of playfulness
in their relationships. One couple told me that they
often play "doctor" together. "I'm the doctor and I'm
going to give her an exam," explains the husband,
"then we switch and she takes over. What we're really
doing is experiencing the excitement of the 'forbidden'
that we had as kids—but it is a helluva lot more fun,"
he says with total seriousness. Another valuable
dimension to the playful side of fantasy lies in the
story of the man who suggested to his timid bride that
she give his penis a name. "Have a conversation with
him," he gently urged her, "get to know him!" The
easy playfulness and good humor in her husband's
idea allowed Paula to feel less inhibited about her
husband's body—and her own—and eventually

allowed her to communicate her own sexual needs more easily.

The basis of fantasy is imagination, and for many couples, the freedom to use their imaginations freely can be one of the most liberating, exciting aspects of lovemaking. Imagination can spark romance and rekindle it. Using your imagination can be as simple as lighting two candles by your bed, making love in the shower or changing your cologne. If you're interested in exploring your imagination you can also simply indulge yourselves in mildly erotic daydreams and share them with each other or you can go all the way to performing the most intricate and detailed scenarios complete with real props and scripts.

Fantasy is based on imagination but talking about or acting on your secret wishes and desires requires trust and complete cooperation from your partner. If you are interested in pursuing or acting on your fantasies— not just keeping them in your head—you must be totally open with each other. Each of you must be willing to enter into the other's fantasy. If you are simply trying to accommodate your partner there will be little pleasure in acting out your fantasies—for either of you.

If you are interested in fantasy but are timid about it, here are some very basic suggestions that a number of couples gave as easy takeoff points:

Tell your fantasies to your partner or write them down in detail. Reading fantasies aloud to each other can be a terrific turn-on and can greatly help in communicating desires and needs that you might have difficulty in expressing in a more direct way.

Try role-playing. Outline a character that you would like to be and then imagine you are that person making love to your partner (who also gets to play out his/her fantasy character at another time). Give yourself a new name and a new personality. You might even dress up as the person whose role you've assumed and construct scripts or scenarios that you want to act out.

Imagine that you are having "an affair" with your own wife or husband. Some couples with whom I spoke actually make clandestine rendezvous in hotels or motels and make mad, passionate love on time stolen from the office and/or household chores.

Imagine that your partner is a total stranger. Construct a complete new identity for him or her including a new name and a whole new personality. Then make love to this exciting stranger and see what develops . . .

Create an imaginary environment where you would enjoy making love: a beach by moonlight, a fragrant, flower-filled meadow, a sleeper on the Orient Express as it hurtles through the dark night to Istanbul. Describe the scene to your partner and make love as you might if you were actually there.

How Far Is Too Far in Fantasy?

Here is an unusual story that was told to me by a vivacious young woman named Maria whom I met at a lecture not long ago. She had asked if I were going to include anything on "fantasy sex" in my next book and, when I said yes, she told me the following experience.

"A friend of mine and I were going to the theater. She had been invited to a cocktail party and, since there was time before the opening curtain, she suggested that we both go. It was the kind of New York party that brings together a lot of different types who would probably never see each other again. . . . An attractive man who looked like a banker in his horn-rimmed glasses and gray flannel suit introduced himself and asked if he could get me a drink. In fact he actually was a banker with a terrific sense of humor and loads of charm and I found myself very much looking forward to the dinner date we later agreed on for the following week.

"Several months later our relationship had developed to the point where I thought I might be in love with Ed and he felt the same way about me. We were thinking of marriage and decided to live together for a while before we actually made it legal. One night, not long after we'd settled into my apartment, he brought home the loveliest silk camisole and bikini pants—lavender satin with delicate ecru lace. I had them on when we made love and he was especially delighted. We laughed about the big turn-on the underwear had produced for both of us and I playfully made him model the bikinis for me. The reaction was terrific—we made love again and again throughout the night.

"Underwear began to play a bigger part in our sex life. Finally Ed told me that he fantasized a lot about wearing women's underwear and he had been afraid to tell me but now he trusted me and felt I would

153

understand. At that point I was still intrigued that this outwardly conservative banker had such eccentric sexual tastes, and since the underwear seemed to excite both of us so much I didn't think there was anything wrong. I even bought him some black lace underpants.

"After a while I got tired of playing with lingerie and suggested that we could try making love without props, but Ed couldn't get an erection unless he wore some kind of lingerie. We tried talking about it but all he would say was that he thought he had finally found someone who could understand him and why was I so unhappy with sex when underwear turned me on, too? Yes, I had enjoyed sex with him, I explained, and I was not against underwear or fantasy or almost anything else that he might enjoy but it bothered me that he insisted on the underwear. Our lovemaking had become one-dimensional and it even frightened me a little. I finally felt it was time to discuss this with someone and I encouraged Ed to see the doctor I spoke with too. Unfortunately, he was not interested and so I eventually left him and his fantasies . . ."

"This story is not as unusual as you might think and points up several interesting aspects of acting out a fantasy. It also helps to explain what may be 'too far' or 'too much,'" observed a therapist with whom I had discussed Ed and Maria's experience. Although at first it had seemed quite out of the ordinary to her, Maria was willing to enter into Ed's fantasy world. Indeed she even encouraged him by giving him "props." Yet there did not appear to be a reciprocal exchange of fantasies; what, if any, were Maria's fantasies and what were her sexual needs? Maria and Ed's fantasy, bizarre as it might seem to many people, was originally exciting to both of them but it became negative and unpleasurable when Ed began to insist that the fantasy be enacted every time they made love. Maria recognized that her own sexual needs covered a broad spectrum, including, but not limited to, acting out sexual fantasies. She perceived Ed's insistence on wearing lingerie as "unhealthy" and sought out the counsel of a qualified professional.

How far, then, is too far in fantasy? Therapists and clinical researchers pretty much agree that anything that two people do together that is *mutually pleasurable* is okay, but most recommend that a couple have a solid history of good communication and complete trust in each other if they wish to act out fantasies.

A word here for those who are non-fantasizers. If, due to lack of interest, or for any other reason, fantasy is not your cup of tea, don't feel pressured to produce a fantasy or to become involved with someone else's. As in every other aspect of lovemaking, the choice is up to you.

If sexual fantasies are not for you, you might be interested in what a good friend of mine labels "loving fantasies." Loving fantasies take work, planning and sometimes props and money, but I assure you, from personal experience, that they are well worth the trouble! Perhaps the following example will help to explain what I mean.

When we were first married I asked my husband what his true fantasies were.

"I have only one," he said without a moment's

hesitation, "to be kidnapped and taken on a slow boat to a desert island—by you."

That year, Valentine's Day fell on a Thursday night, and I asked Norman to be home by six, we'd be having a "special dinner." When he arrived, the house was lit with small, shimmering candles and Edith Piaf was singing "La Vie en Rose."

"What's happening?" he asked.

"A surprise," I said, leading him to the living room where we started to sip some chilled champagne. After we talked for a few minutes the doorbell rang.

"Why don't you answer it?" I suggested sweetly.

As he went to the front door, I gathered up all my things and ran out the back.

Norman found two men wearing masks on the steps. "Put on your overcoat," one ordered gruffly, "And take a scarf—it's cold," commanded the other. Norman, fearless, responded, "Oh, Edward, it's you . . ."

"You don't know me," Edward said gruffly, and added, "Don't say anything, this is my fantasy too."

Norman, dressed warmly, was guided to a car parked in front of our door, and driven through dark, deserted streets to the south end of Manhattan where he would be taken by boat to his fantasy island.

Waiting with a picnic basket and two tokens in hand, I greeted him at the gate to the Staten Island Ferry. The kidnappers released him into my custody and we dined on Brie, crusty bread, Westphalian ham and red wine as the boat pulled away from the dock and we watched the magnificent downtown skyline recede into the distance.

Fantasy

When we got back to Manhattan, it was near eleven o'clock and the car was waiting to make one more fantasy come true. We took a ride uptown and drove through Central Park and then slowly toward 59th Street.

"Where are we going?" asked Norman, always curious.

"You'll see," I said mysteriously as we pulled up to the side door of Bloomingdale's where the guard unlocked the door for us. He pulled a switch and suddenly lights flooded Norman's favorite place in New York, Swensen's ice cream parlor, where we were let loose to gorge ourselves on every kind of frozen delight imaginable.

"How did you ever pull this one off?" Norman asked, between bites of Swiss orange chocolate, almond, coconut and banana.

"Never question a fantasy," I replied, sampling the pistachio and butter crunch.

The kidnapping was several years ago and I won't reveal how Norman really one-upped me on *my* fantasy last year, but I can guarantee that it's worth it to make someone's dreams come true.

15
OUTSIDE EXPERIMENTS

The word used to be ADULTERY. Then it became
INFIDELITY. Now it's EXTRA-MARITAL or CO-MARITAL sex
and statistics show that it's at an all-time high. The
issue here is not whether it's right or wrong but *why* a
man or a woman wants to indulge in "outside" sex of
whatever kind—group, menage à trois, or classical
one-to-one—and if he or she *does*, what can you do
about it.

First, it's enlightening to look at still another basic
difference in attitudes between men and women. Men
whom I interviewed often made a distinction between
the "one-night stand" and "an affair." "A one-night
stand is strictly for sex," is the way an Indianapolis
man defined it. "I may not even know her name. An
affair is when you have an ongoing relationship with
someone. An affair gives you something, something
that you probably are missing at home." Women, too,

make this distinction between sex-only and sex-with-caring, but the casual, strictly-for-sex kind of extramarital encounter often seems to lead to something deeper. "What started out as a pure physical joyride for me quickly turned into a strong attachment because I was using sex as a substitute for other things missing in my marriage," says a woman who carefully analyzed the reasons for the breakup of her seventeen-year marriage.

The underlying difference in attitude or concept about extramarital sex is a familiar one. Many men told me they can enjoy purely physical sex with little or no emotional involvement while most women, although they can imagine sex without emotional contact, find it difficult to accept in reality. "I can't bear to think of my husband kissing another woman, even if it's a prostitute," admits a suburban housewife. To her, kissing means some kind of emotional attachment or commitment but many men would disagree. "Good sex—no strings attached—is simply good sex. It's like a massage," says a lawyer who is often away from home on business. "It feels great to your body and doesn't interfere with your marriage."

What, then, is infidelity? The definition often varies from person to person and couple to couple, but men generally consider infidelity to mean "an affair," that is, a relationship that is more than "just sex," while women generally conceive of infidelity as any kind of extramarital sexual contact, no matter how fleeting. Thus it's a wise idea to clearly define your particular concept of "faithfulness" for your partner. Once you know each other's attitudes and ideas you'll both be far better equipped to avoid any problems that may arise in this sensitive area. You can offset anxieties and difficulties by honestly examining how you each feel about faithfulness and agreeing on what it is that you both want from your relationship.

Experts as well as the couples interviewed generally agreed that men and women who enjoy sexual and emotional intimacy have little need for extramarital sex—unless there are specific circumstances such as extended travel or illness of one partner. To put it plainly: when you're in love with someone, being faithful is not a problem. If it becomes an effort, common sense would tell you "there's trouble here," and the best response is to first examine why you no longer feel satisfied at home.

"No one is immune from impure thoughts," says an exceptionally attractive Hollywood actor of 35 who has been married for eight years. "The real question is whether you act on them. Ask yourself: *What is the risk? What are the consequences?* I, for one, know that I'm not going to mess up my marriage for, excuse my language, a piece of ass, no matter how tempting it is." "You are not responsible for your feelings," affirms a behavioral therapist, "you are responsible for your actions." "Look, but don't touch," is the way another woman who values her marriage states the case for fidelity.

If It Happens . . .

"What do you do when you find a note from another woman in your husband's jacket pocket?" was a question that was put to a psychologist on a recent radio program where she and I were appearing as guests. "I found out that my wife was playing around when I got herpes, what should I do?" was another difficult query. Solutions to these intensely painful problems must be worked out by the individuals involved, but experts offer some guidelines that might be helpful.

First, carefully examine your own feelings and your relationship. The man who left the note in his pocket might be trying unconsciously to tell his wife: "I'm involved with another woman and I am letting you know so that we can do something about it." Or he may be saying: "I left the note in my pocket because I'm very angry at you and I'm trying to get back at you by having an affair."

Each person has his or her deep-rooted reasons for "playing around," but therapists point out that certain recurrent themes are sounded by men and women who seek extramarital sex. The most common are; the need for intimacy, loneliness, boredom, the need for novelty, unrealistic expectations, the assurance that one is still desirable, the need to be with someone who does not know one's faults or weaknesses. Some observers of human behavior feel that men especially are prone to extramarital sex. "Males often have contradictory feelings about monogamy," says one perceptive Los Angeles graduate student. "There's a need for home and hearth but there's also the early conditioning to 'score' as often as possible. This can continue to be a powerful pull even in a very satisfactory marriage."

It's crucial that you don't lie to yourself when considering a situation involving extramarital sex. Ask yourself why you need to go outside the marriage, what is lacking in your relationship, why you cannot discuss the situation with your partner. These are deep and searching questions which involve the entire fabric of your life with your husband or wife. Don't hesitate to seek professional counsel to help you answer them.

If your partner is the one who is, or has been, involved with outside sex, concentrate on the same issues: Why has he or she gone outside the marriage? What is it that your partner may be needing that you haven't given him or her?

Don't torture yourself or your husband or wife with questions about what the other person looked like or how they were in bed. Concentrate instead on *why* you could not satisfy your partner's needs and why your partner could not speak honestly with you. It is ultimately your choice whether to ignore the situation—or face it, and reevaluate your marriage, perhaps seeking help to make it stronger and revitalize a commitment that has ebbed away.

Obviously the best time to communicate about a problem is *before* anything happens. Some men and women who have a strong commitment to their marriage but recognize the warning signals tell their partners they are thinking of extramarital sex. Such openness can often lead to a re-examination of your mutual needs and desires and make for a stronger, deeper bond.

One woman I know suspected her husband of having an affair, and after much self-searching confronted him—not with angry accusations—but with how much she loved and needed him. He said that he had indeed contemplated becoming involved with another woman because he had not felt truly loved and needed, and that he had had no idea of the depth and intensity of her commitment to him, as she had never expressed herself so directly before. This painful revelation and the honest, open discussion that it sparked was the beginning of real intimacy in their marriage.

If your husband or wife finds out about your affair or if you tell your partner what has happened, don't expect instant understanding or forgiveness. Realize that there are many painful phases to be weathered. "When he first told me I was in unbelievable pain. I remember vividly that I had to go to a crucial meeting at the office and my hands were shaking so much that I couldn't put my lipstick on. I just wanted to get out of the house," said one woman whose husband told her the reason for his wandering was that he was not receiving the kind of sexuality he needed at home. "Afterward, I felt rage. I wanted to hit him and hurt him physically. Instead I withdrew and didn't say anything for days and then I went through the whole range of feelings over and over until they lost their edge and I began to want to be with him. It took two weeks of talking, talking, talking until we made love and I began to think of trusting him again."

This pattern of pain/anger/withdrawal is one that should not be suppressed or speeded-up. The complete process is necessary for, unless they are dealt with, these deep and destructive feelings can easily preclude the rebuilding of a healthy and loving relationship.

The person who finds out that his mate has been unfaithful suffers a tremendous loss of dignity and self-esteem. Recognize that rebuilding trust and confidence and intimacy takes time and love and a great deal of sensitivity. Without being heavy-handed about it, let your partner know where you will be and when you'll be home—don't make him or her ask. If you're going to be late, telephone and say where you are and when you'll return. If you can include your partner in your plans, so much the better. Ask what it is that you can do to help him or her trust you again— and then do it consistently.

There will still be times of hurt and anger—on both sides—but if the relationship is going to change and improve, you will have to express a great deal of love and willingness to nurture each other.

16

INTERFERENCES:
How to Cope with In-Laws, Kids, Money, Careers . . .

"It's great to talk about all this passion and romance and seduction stuff," a young woman in a TV studio audience declared, *"but if your mother-in-law is in the next room, it's not going to work. . . ."* And it's not going to work if your children are climbing into bed with you, if your checkbook is overdrawn, if you've just had your fifth run-in with your boss or today's sales projections missed the mark. Kids, in-laws, money and careers are major interferences when it comes to maintaining an intense, meaningful relationship.

CHILDREN

A strong relationship is a delicate balance of two
equals who are deeply committed to each other in
every way. Perhaps the most unbalancing factor in any
relationship is the birth of a child. Some recent studies
point to the fact that couples without children are
happier than those with families. This is consistently
underscored by the men and women I interviewed
who felt that their marriages were exceptionally sound
in large measure because they had no children.
Obviously people aren't going to stop having
offspring; the question is, how to adjust to them while
maintaining a vital and intimate relationship.

Most experts and couples agree that the years from
one to five are the most difficult for parents. Children's
physical demands are at their highest and, at the same
time, mothers and fathers are having to make major
emotional and financial adjustments. "One of the keys
to coping with children is to never forget that they are
additions to a marriage," observes a woman who works
at home and also mothers two young daughters. "You
must remember that you and your husband are the
basic unit and the kids expand that core, they don't
divide it." A well-known New York art director with a
fifteen-month-old son says, "I always keep in mind
what my mother used to tell me, 'Your father comes
first.' Sometimes I was jealous but I had to respect
her."

If you want your marriage to survive you've got to
make time to be alone together on a regular basis.

There are a number of creative ways couples can achieve this. "My neighbors take my kids one Sunday afternoon and we take theirs the next," says an office manager/mother from Minneapolis. "Early on I established a marvelous habit," explains another woman. "I ship the kids to my mother-in-law's every Friday night. She loves having them and Jack and I feel we're doing all of us a favor." "A night at the local Holiday Inn at least once or twice a month is what keeps us together," claims a husband who initiated the practice at the advice of his minister.

"A lock on the door is an invaluable tool for keeping passion alive," points out a San Francisco psychologist who also suggests, "Put a note up saying, 'Private time,' or fly a flag if you have to, but tell the kids not to disturb you—unless it's an emergency—for an hour or as long as they can take it. Give them a new toy, turn on the TV, and you'll soon find they'll adjust to your needs instead of vice-versa."

IN-LAWS

"Jim's just a bit stingy when it comes to carving the roast, isn't he?" observes Marilyn's mother as they do the dishes together. Remarks like these are apt to create a certain tension in the bedroom later on. In-laws such as Marilyn's mother have always had bad press and much of it seems to be justified. A parent who is constantly trying to maintain control or who has nothing much else to do except offer criticism is an unwelcome addition to even the most stable relationship.

Most couples who successfully handle one (or more) intrusive in-laws say that by facing the situation early, many of the blooming problems can be nipped in the bud. "Charles and I finally realized that we had to take a united stand," says Suzanne, whose Southern mother-in-law felt the need to comment sweetly on everything from her cooking to her hair color. If mother said "Northerners really can't do a pecan pie," or "Isn't it a shame, darling, that your little ones don't understand the meaning of manners," both Suzanne and Charles would firmly but politely suggest that Mom might find more palatable pastry or more mannerly children at another location. Mrs. B—, seeing an impregnable unity, finally ceased commenting. "If it's a choice between your wife and your parents," says Grace, a wise and loving mother-in-law whom I know, "the choice should be obvious."

MONEY

"Money and sex are the two biggest trouble spots in a marriage," says a New York divorce lawyer. "If you have a lot of both there's no problem, but that is not the usual case." "I can talk freely about the most intimate aspects of my life," admits a successful businessman, "but I clam up when it comes to money.

170

My wife doesn't even know what's in the bank account."

Few people would deny the dangers and delights inherent in money. Thousands of books have been written on the subject and millions of arguments center on it. Attitudes about money can often reveal a great deal about the state of a marriage. An equal partnership can't exist if information is being withheld about money, or if one partner is doing all the money managing without the participation of the other. Even if only one person in the relationship is working, both of you must be responsible for understanding your financial affairs. The wife who says, "He's doing all the earning so it's right he does all the investing," or the husband who claims "She's the one who takes care of the checkbook" are in for trouble. Each of you should insist on knowing what your money situation is and each should take an equal responsibility for negotiating any needs that arise.

CAREERS

Closely related to money matters are careers. The two-career family is becoming the norm and, as ambitions rise, so can the problems in any relationship. Two lawyers who were recently married felt they had the best of all possible worlds. "We were in the same profession with almost equal salaries and we shared the same goals," says Nancy. "At first there were no conflicts, but then I had to do a lot of week-night entertaining and my husband needed to spend long weekend hours at the law library. We rarely saw each other. Added to that we began to think of having a child, but I felt that my career would fall way behind if I became pregnant. I finally saw that even though we believed we were the ideal couple we were actually locked in an intense, destructive competition."

Awareness of the problem was the beginning of its solution. These two lawyers who negotiated complex settlements for clients every day had been reluctant to apply their skills to their own relationship. It took months of talking and setting priorities and understanding what really made their lives together tick—other than their jobs—to pull the marriage back together again.

Kids, in-laws, money and careers are obvious interferences, but I would add another to this list, not as monumental perhaps, but nevertheless an insidious troublemaker: television. "It's ten o'clock, the kids are tucked into bed, you've just slid into silky clean sheets and the set goes on. Television, that's what today's love-killer is," says a wise woman whose marriage has survived every modern inconvenience. She and her husband turn off the tube, tune out the world, pour themselves a glass of sherry—and talk.

17
KNOWING AND DOING

After reading this book you may be tempted to say, "But I know most of these things," and it's true that much of what's here appears to be simple and just plain common sense, yet

> when was the last time you sent her a rose? When was the last time you brought him coffee and orange juice in bed? When was the last time you read a book together, played tennis together, took a bath together? When was the last time you talked and talked and talked until the sun came up?

If there's one message that comes through from men and women who have made something very special of their lives together, it's this:

Set aside the time to understand each other and to do the things that make your relationship work—and then *do* them.